Primary special needs and the National Curriculum

This book addresses the issues and practicalities of implementing
the National Curriculum at classroom level in primary schools.
The approach is pragmatic – we have a National Curriculum and
we must use it to foster progress for children who find school-
based learning difficult.

Implementing the National Curriculum is discussed in relation
to the need for safegarding a broad curriculum, assessing children's learning, and helping all children to gain access to the
National Curriculum. There are implications also for the classroom grouping of children, making the best use of resources
(including Special Educational Needs co-ordinators, classmates,
care-givers, support services, and materials) and record-keeping.
These areas are explored in the light of both classroom practice
and research evidence. Ann Lewis also offers guidelines on how to
carry out SATs with children who have difficulties in learning, and
examines the legal position concerning exceptions from the
National Curriculum.

Ann Lewis is a lecturer in Primary Education at the University of
Warwick, and has taught in primary and special schools. She has
been involved extensively in the development of curricula for
children with learning difficulties. She is one of the editors of
Education 3-13, and a member of the Editorial Committee for
Special Children.

Primary special needs and the National Curriculum

Ann Lewis

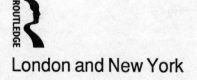

London and New York

First published 1991
by Routledge
11 New Fetter Lane, London EC4P 4EE

Simultaneously published in the USA and Canada
by Routledge
a division of Routledge, Chapman and Hall, Inc.
29 West 35th Street, New York, NY 10001

Typeset by LaserScript Limited, Mitcham, Surrey
Printed in Great Britain by
Biddles Ltd, Guildford and King's Lynn

British Library Cataloguing in Publication Data

Lewis, Ann *1950–*
    Primary special needs and the National Curriculum.
    1. Great Britain. Primary schools. Slow learning students.
    Remedial education
    I. Title
    371.926720941

0-415-05427-3
0-415-05428-1 pbk

Library of Congress Cataloging-in-Publication Data
0-415-05427-3
0-415-05428-1 pbk
Has been applied for

Dumb Insolence

I'm big for ten years old
Maybe that's why they get at me

Teachers, parents, cops
Always getting at me

When they get at me

I don't hit em
They can do you for that

I don't swear at em
They can do you for that

I stick my hands in my pockets
And stare at them

And while I stare at them
I think about sick

They call it dumb insolence

They don't like it
But they can't do you for it

I've been done before
They say if I get done again

They'll put me in a home
So I do dumb insolence

Adrian Mitchell

Source: Roger McGough (1981) *Strictly Private*, Harmondsworth: Penguin

Contents

Figures and tables

Acknowledgements

Many people have contributed indirectly to this book and my thanks go to them all. The ideas have been shaped by the multifarious children, students and colleagues with whom I have worked in London, the West Midlands and the USA. My thanks in particular to Jim Campbell, Tricia David, Lois Thorpe and Liz Wain who have read parts or all of the book in draft. Their constructive criticism and enthusiasm have been instrumental in my completing the manuscript. My special thanks to Gerry for his tolerance, continuing encouragement and incisive comments on draft versions. I am grateful to Simon for permission to include copies of his 'Fairy Liquid' writing, to Jason Yeomans for the cover photograph, to the DES for clarification concerning regulations for temporary exceptions and to Helen Fairlie and Sue Joshua at Routledge for their editorial support.

The poem 'Dumb Insolence' is reproduced by permission of Roger McGough and figure 7.1 is reproduced by permission of HMSO. Part of chapter 8 was published in *Special Children* (issue 25, November 1988) and is included here with the permission of Howard Sharron.

Abbreviations

AT(s)	Attainment Target(s)
CACE	Central Advisory Council for Education
CATS	Consortium for Assessment and Testing in Schools
ERA	1988 Education Reform Act
DES	Department of Education and Science
HMI	Her Majesty's Inspectorate (of schools)
LEA	Local Education Authority
LMS	Local Management of Schools
NC	National Curriculum
NCC	National Curriculum Council
NFER	National Foundation for Educational Research
PC	Profile Component
PMLD	Profound and Multiple Learning Difficulties
POS(s)	Programme(s) of Study
SAT(s)	Standard Assessment Task(s)
SDP	School Development Plans
SEAC	School Examinations and Assessment Council
SEN	Special Educational Needs
SLD	Severe Learning Difficulties
SOA(s)	Statement(s) of Attainment
STAIR	Standard Tests and Assessment Implementation Research
TGAT	Task Group on Assessment and Testing
TIPS	Teacher Information Packs
WO	Welsh Office

Chapter 1

Introduction

The aim of this book is to address the issues and practicalities of implementing the National Curriculum (NC) at classroom level in mainstream primary schools. The approach is pragmatic: we have an NC and we must use it to foster progress for children who find school-based learning difficult. Some of these children may have statements of special educational needs (SEN) but most are likely to be without the protection, or millstone, depending on one's ideological stance, of a statement.

The NC is a statement of educational entitlement to which no child should be denied. To withdraw a child's entitlement by disapplying the NC requires strong justification. There is, despite some initial confusion, no ambiguity in the various NC documents about the broad situation for children with learning difficulties. These children, if they are in maintained schools, should participate in the NC. It is not the case, as has been reported incorrectly, that the NC is automatically disapplied for all children with statements or children attending special schools.

At the consultation stage there were many reservations about the suitability and practicability of the proposed NC in relation to children with SEN (Simon 1988, Haviland 1988, Wedell 1988). Later commentators, reflecting on the 1988 Education Reform Act (ERA), of which the NC is a part, have confirmed reservations about the NC and children with SEN (e.g. Kelly 1990).

Teachers in mainstream schools have also been concerned about including children with SEN within the framework of the NC. In one survey (Wragg *et al.* 1989) over three-quarters of the 901 primary teachers questioned considered that including children with SEN in the NC would be difficult or very difficult. Similarly, identifying children's learning difficulties was anticipated as

difficult or very difficult by approximately twothirds of the teachers. The data does not show to what extent these perceptions
were caused by the implementation of the NC itself. It may have
been the case that these teachers were concerned about working
with children with SEN and identifying learning difficulties regardless of the additional demands of the NC. A review by HMI of
special needs issues (HMI 1990a) suggests that teachers' concerns
may have been well-founded. Reviewing special needs issues over
the decade since the Warnock Report (DES 1978a), HMI concluded: 'It is clear that some primary ... schools will need to review
their provision for pupils with SEN if they are to ensure that these
pupils have full access to the National Curriculum' (para. 58).

LEARNING DIFFICULTIES

This book is about adapting and developing the NC with children
who experience difficulties in school-based learning. The concept
of learning difficulties has proved difficult to pin down. It is used
in different ways by practitioners, researchers and administrators
and, even within these groups, interpretations differ (Hegarty
1987, Wolfendale 1987, Norwich 1990). Difficulties in learning
may stem from factors within the child, such as poor short term
memory, and/or from a mismatch between the learning opportunities which children need and the educational experiences
which are being provided.

This stance is reflected in the NCC's (1989a) statement that,
'Special educational needs are not just a reflection of pupils'
inherent difficulties or disabilities; they are often related to factors
within schools which can prevent or exacerbate problems' (para.
5). This statement stresses that SEN and, within these, learning
difficulties, are not purely within the child. A child's learning
difficulties may be more or less problematic for the teacher,
depending on the ways in which the school responds to the child.
This is not to deny that difficulties in learning exist but highlights
that contributing causes may lie in the classroom.

Many researchers have tried to identify whether or not children
who have difficulties in school-based learning are different from
other children in terms of effective teaching approaches. It has
been asked whether these children are just 'delayed' or
qualitatively 'different' from other children in the ways in which
they learn. This is an important question for teachers. Should a

9-year old with reading difficulties, reading at the level of a typical 7-year old, be taught in the same way as normal 7-year olds? To answer 'yes' to this question would be to imply that the first child is delayed but not qualitatively different in his or her learning needs from those of the second child.

The evidence from both practice and research is that, unsurprisingly, children with learning difficulties are a heterogeneous group. An extensive review of research on learner and teacher characteristics (Cronbach and Snow 1977) concluded that it is impossible to make firm generalisations about certain teaching methods being more effective than others for 'low ability' children. There was, for example, no support for teaching children with learning difficulties solely through a didactic, step by step method. However, the review did provide qualified support for the view that children with learning difficulties benefit more from didactic methods than from guided learning whereas the reverse tends to be the case for able children. The implication is that children with difficulties in learning need a mixture of teaching approaches with a bias towards fairly structured methods.

One reason for the failure of research to come up with 'best buys' in terms of teaching methods specifically orientated to children with difficulties in learning, as a group, is the heterogenity of that group. One broad theoretical distinction within the group has been between children who are generally 'slow' compared with peers, and children who have a specific learning difficulty in one or several areas but otherwise have average or above-average attainments compared with peers (Rutter and Yule 1975). Work over the last decade has endeavoured to identify specific subgroups of specific learning difficulties and there is evidence that it may be valid to distinguish between children with language, visual–spatial, or 'mixed processing deficits' (Tyler 1990). However, even if we could make these kinds of distinction with certainty, there remains the question of how best to teach these various groups of children. As yet there are no unequivocally 'best' methods based on specific diagnoses. Flexibility in teaching methods, careful monitoring of the child's learning, and the encouragement of a broad range of learning strategies remain important characteristics of effective teaching for all children.

The need for differentiation of teaching methods does not imply differentiation of curricular aims. For example, it is appropriate to have as an educational aim for all children that they become fluent readers, and we may want all children to read fluently fiction, poetry and reference books, but the way in which we help children to achieve this will reflect differences between the children. One child may gain this fluency almost unaided whereas another child may need intermittent adult guidance and encouragement, while a third child may need direct and frequent teaching.

POTENTIAL STRENGTHS OF THE NATIONAL CURRICULUM FOR CHILDREN WITH LEARNING DIFFICULTIES

There are a number of aspects of the NC which could be very beneficial for children with learning difficulties. The shared curricular framework means that, potentially, those children are more likely to be working within mainstream classes alongside peers. Previously, SEN work has often been seen as different in both content and kind from activities carried out by other children. Some commentators (Dessent 1987, Moore and Morrison 1988) have argued that the separation of special needs 'experts' has reinforced these perceived differences. The emphasis on a common curriculum is important both within mainstream schools (encouraging children with mild or moderate learning difficulties to be taught within the mainstream class) and between special and mainstream schools.

The NC also provides a shared curricular language. Teachers know roughly what is meant when a child is described as having worked on (say) English targets 3 and 4 at level 2, whether we are talking about a child involved in a mainstream class full-time, in withdrawal group work or in activities in a special school. By comparison, to be told that a child is on (say) book 3 of a certain scheme is only meaningful if the listener is familiar with that particular scheme.

The NC should also lead to primary aged children with difficulties in learning receiving a broad curriculum encompassing not just language, literacy, mathematics and RE but also science, technology, geography, history, music, art and PE. In the past the curricula for children with learning difficulties, in mainstream and special schools, have been criticised as being too restricted and concentrating on narrow teaching of 'basic' skills (ILEA 1985a, DES 1986).

Another positive feature of the NC in relation to children with learning difficulties is the acknowledged importance of assessing children's learning at regular intervals; seeing this as being tied into teaching rather than as an 'add-on' to measure only end-products of learning. Assessment of children's learning has been an important part of special needs work. This is illustrated in the use of diagnostic tests at regular intervals (e.g. simple tests of specific phonic skills) and the development of techniques such as curriculum-based assessment. The assessments required in the NC are an extension of these approaches.

THE IMPORTANCE OF COLLECTIVE RESPONSIBILITY FOR CHILDREN WITH LEARNING DIFFICULTIES

Collective (i.e. whole school) responsibility for meeting children's individual needs has been advocated for some time (e.g. Wolfendale 1987, Ainscow and Florek 1989). Such collective responsibility has repercussions for all aspects of the school. These have been discussed by Tony Dessent (1987) who acknowledges the 'enormous challenge' to many schools. He concludes that a school's educational philosophy may not always be conducive to a whole school approach to planning for SEN, in which case it will take many small and gradual moves to work towards acceptance of this collective responsibility.

Many primary schools now have a designated teacher with an interest in, and responsibility for, SEN (this is discussed further in chapter 8), but it will be to the detriment of children's individual needs if this leads other staff to feel that children with SEN are not their responsibility. A large minority of children (approximately 20 per cent of all children according to the Warnock Report [DES 1978a]) have some special individual teaching/learning needs at some time during their school careers. This means that all teachers need to be prepared to foster the learning of these children.

Before the NC was in place, Sheila Wolfendale, Tony Dessent and others were advocating collective school responsibility for children with difficulties in learning. This has been given an extra boost by the wider development of School Development Plans (Hargreaves *et al.* 1989) as a mechanism for the implementation and development of the NC. The requirements of children with learning difficulties are one element within this overall planning. It is likely to be more effective if the concern about providing for children with difficulties in learning runs through all documents than if it is considered only in separate policy documents. A fruitful approach is to think about how the school promotes the differentiation of the curriculum, rather than identifying children with learning difficulties as a particular group. There is a danger that, by focusing specifically on children with learning difficulties, they become seen as invariably needing something different from other children. What is needed is the recognition and acceptance of individuality applied to all children.

However, whole school policies on learning difficulties may be only a façade, masking rather than confronting the issues by recording on paper policies and statements of principles but not translating these into practice. They may also not necessarily be a way of promoting good practice but may instead encourage highly individualised and segregated provision within the school. Thus, while collective responsibility for children with learning difficulties is important in principle, the approaches embodied in that collective responsibility need critical evaluation. At present, finding time to discuss matters such as the provision of equal opportunities, including those for children with learning difficulties, may be genuinely difficult when schools are already having to review their entire curricula.

AN INTEGRATED CURRICULUM

One way of visualising the whole school curriculum, including the curriculum for children with learning difficulties, is as a ladder in which broad steps are specified for all children. Within this broad ladder there are points at which, for some children and possibly for only some of the time, smaller intermediate rungs are needed. Like most analogies this ladder model has some weaknesses, such as an image of children's learning as necessarily hierarchical, clearly defined, and sequential. However, the ladder idea does emphasise the integration of curricula for all children, curricular progression and continuity, and fits with the concept of ten broad levels of attainment that is embodied in the NC.

The NC is a curriculum for all children and this book is about the strategies which teachers might use to give all children access to that curriculum. Many of the examples given relate to the core subjects but the strategies could be applied across all curricular areas. Despite the positive stance of this introduction, there are some worrying aspects of the NC and these are discussed in the relevant chapters. The following two chapters focus on the range of the curriculum for children with difficulties in learning. This is discussed first as a general issue (chapter 2) and then in relation to implications for practice (chapter 3).

Chapter 2

Safeguarding a broad curriculum

At the heart of the ERA lies a contradiction. Sections 1 and 2 of the Act reflect contrasting approaches to aims and content in education. Section 1 is broad, referring to the need for a curriculum which promotes 'spiritual, moral, cultural, mental and physical development' and prepares pupils for the 'opportunities, responsibilities and experiences of adult life'. By contrast, Section 2 of the Act discusses the planned outlines of work in the discrete foundation subjects (plus RE). Section 2 is, overwhelmingly, addressing only part of the aims given in Section 1; the broader aims are not met by the statutory programmes of study (POSs).

There have been attempts to bridge this gap in two ways. First, it has been stated (e.g. NCC 1989b) that subject-specific POSs, attainment targets (ATs) and assessment arrangements do not constitute the whole curriculum. A child's whole curriculum should be wider than these in order to meet the aims of Section 1 of the ERA. The NCC's Curriculum Guidence 3 is categorical about this: 'The National Curriculum alone will not provide the necessary breadth' (NCC 1990a:1). Second, cross-curricular strategies have gained increasing prominence. Cross-curricular strategies encompass: dimensions (e.g. equal opportunities) which are 'concerned with the intentional promotion of personal and social development through the curriculum as a whole' (NCC 1989b: para. 9); skills (referred to as 'competencies' in the early NC documentation), such as numeracy and personal skills, which are developed through several different aspects of the curriculum; and themes (e.g. citizenship, environmental education) which are essential parts of the whole curriculum but which may straddle one or more of the foundation subjects. For example, elements of citizenship feature in geography and history POSs. Themes could also go beyond the basic curriculum of the foundation subjects and RE. To continue the example of citizenship, this might reasonably include the development of a caring attitude towards others. There has been considerable variation in which topics have been identified as themes in successive NC documents. Citizenship, which at first did not appear, is now one of the five 'pre-eminent' (NCC 1990a) themes.

One problem with these two attempts at bridging the gap between Sections 1 and 2 of the ERA is that, while subject-specific POSs, ATs and assessment arrangements are statutory, much cross-curricular work and all work outside the non-'basic curriculum' are only advisory. NCC recognised the ambiguous position of the cross-curricular themes: 'Where these themes are embedded in the NC POSs they are statutory' but 'Other aspects, while not statutory, are clearly required if schools are to provide an education which promotes the aims defined in section 1 of the ERA' (NCC 1989b: para. 16). This is an important issue for those concerned with teaching children who have difficulties in learning. Their aims often emphasise developing children's self-confidence and enthusiasm for learning, not attaining specific subject targets.

This creates a potential dilemma which is difficult to resolve. For example, one child may need speech therapy in order to communicate more effectively with others, another child may need small group therapy to help to overcome emotional difficulties and so collaborate with classmates. In both these examples, the prior need will militate against a broad and balanced curriculum, at least in the short term. Yet without specific help the child may be hampered from benefiting from the broader curriculum.

POSSIBLE LIMITATIONS TO A BROAD CURRICULUM FOR CHILDREN WITH DIFFICULTIES IN LEARNING

There are three identifiable forces which are likely to operate to diminish the curricular breadth of the whole curriculum as described in the ERA. These three forces are: uncertainties about the foci of entitlement, differences between the status of subjects because of standard assessment tasks (SATs), and available curriculum time. The first two of these forces are likely to apply more sharply to children with learning difficulties than to other pupils, the third will apply to all children.

An entitlement to what?

It is important to be clear about what is within and what is beyond the NC because of the stress in the ERA that is placed on the NC as an entitlement for all children. This is repeated in the NCC's *Framework for the Primary Curriculum* (NCC 1989c): 'The National Curriculum (which is statutory) is non-negotiable as a framework for every school and as an entitlement for all pupils' (2.5). Klaus Wedell (1989) suggests that Sections 17–19 of the ERA imply that it is only the basic NC, not the whole curriculum, which has to be safeguarded in law. In statutory terms, the basic NC is defined in the Orders containing the POSs. Since these do not contain comprehensive or coherent outlines of cross-curricular work, are the cross-curricular areas excluded from the entitlement curriculum? These kinds of issues may ultimately be decided only through costly and time-consuming case law. Meanwhile it is important that, particularly for children with learning difficulties, the NC is regarded as being as wide as possible and not confined to subject-specific POSs.

SATs: another threat to curriculum breadth?

Early development of SATs focused on the core subjects of English, mathematics and science. However, the letters from the DES to chairs of working groups indicated that it was intended initially that all foundation subjects should be assessed, in part, through nationally prescribed tests. This planned breadth of SATs has since been reduced considerably (see chapter 10). If heads and teachers feel under pressure to be seen to have good results on reported assessments, including SATs, then children with difficulties in learning may come to be regarded as the children who will 'pull down' a school's results. As a consequence there may be a temptation to give those children more work on the core subject attainment targets which are reported and less work on other areas. In wider educational terms this would clearly be undesirable. It may also be counter-productive since, as discussed in chapter 3, broad integrated work may well provide the basis for learning to apply and generalise skills and knowledge, and to maximise children's motivation, thereby indirectly leading to improved attainments.

Before considering how we might meet the demands for

breadth in curriculum content, it is worth reviewing the advice being given to schools concerning time allocations in specific foundation subjects. This affects the curricula for all children, including those with difficulties in learning.

Stated time allocations in NC documents

The consultation document on the NC (DES 1987) tried to map possible timetable allocations for foundation subjects at secondary school level but did not do this for primary schools. It stated only that, 'The *majority of curriculum time* at primary level should be devoted to the core subjects' (para. 14; my emphasis). In the ERA the ten subjects in the basic curriculum have not been given time allocations, either individually or grouped, within a school's time-table. The ERA specifically excluded this and also prevented orders from being made to bring in such time allocations. However, schools do have to spend a 'reasonable time' on foundation subjects so that children carry out 'worthwhile work' (DES 1989a).

There has been much debate about how the term 'reasonable' should be defined but no firm conclusions have been reached and the diversity of school arrangements make this difficult. It may be easy for a school operating a traditional subject-based timetable to say with some certainty that 90 per cent of the school week is timetabled for foundation subjects. It is virtually impossible for a school operating an integrated day and/or an integrated curricu-lum to estimate, either by class or (even more so) by child, how much time has been spent on all or individual foundation subjects. Regulations concerning the curriculum audit (to be completed by headteachers) initially included requests for estimates of planned time to be spent on each foundation subject as well as retrospective accounting of time actually spent. Problems with this were soon apparent and the first set of regulations were withdrawn in January 1990. Revised regulations focused on retrospective reporting only.

The result of this debate about time allocations, and the reason for discussing it in this chapter, is that it leaves heads and teachers with considerable freedom concerning how they plan the curriculum. Although there have been recommendations about time allocations for some individual subjects (generally in interim reports or in letters from the DES to chairs of working parties), these are not part of the legal requirements of the NC. A minimum teaching week (i.e. total lesson time) of 21 hours for reception to year 2 or 23.5 hours for years 3–6 has been recommended (DES 1990a). The following time allocations for individual subjects (taken from the various subject documents) have been suggested within this teaching week:

- English   8 periods per 40-period week
- Maths   20 per cent of total lesson time
- Science (incl. technology)   12.5 per cent of total lesson time
- History   3–4 periods per 40-period week
- Geography   3 periods per 40-period week
- Music   No allocation suggested to date
- Art   No allocation suggested to date
- PE   No allocation suggested to date
- RE   No allocation suggested to date

It is immediately clear that there are several difficulties with these, albeit tentatively, suggested time allocations. First, the different subject groups do not use the same units to define time allocation. Second, the assumed 40-period week reflects a secondary rather than a primary school orientation to defining time allocation.

If these time allocations were put on to the same scale, the results might look something like this:

- English   20 per cent of total lesson time
- Maths   20 per cent of total lesson time
- Science (incl. technology)   12.5 per cent of total lesson time
- History   10 per cent of total lesson time
- Geography   7.5 per cent of total lesson time
- Music   No allocation suggested to date
- Art   No allocation suggested to date
- PE   No allocation suggested to date
- RE   No allocation suggested to date

Thus 70 per cent of the teaching week appears to be taken up by the core subjects, technology, history and geography. This leaves 30 per cent of the teaching week for music, art, PE, RE and all cross-curricular themes where these are taught separately from foundation subjects.

Areas such as art and PE are notoriously time consuming in primary, especially infant, schools. A 30-minute swimming period, for example, could easily occupy 90 minutes if the time required for transporting children to and from an off-site pool and for changing is taken into account. This also illustrates the difficulties of defining time spent on specific curricular areas at primary level. Most teachers take advantage of opportunities such as a bus journey to the swimming baths to develop children's observations of the area, to practise various rhymes or singing games or to talk with individual children.

There will be some monitoring of the NC to check that schools are providing children with 'reasonable time' and so are developing 'worthwhile study' on each of the foundation subjects. A number of LEAs are already beginning to change the structure of their inspectorate/advisory and administrative services to reflect future demands concerning both the monitoring of the NC and the operation of Local Management of Schools (LMS).

The issue of time allocation was highlighted in HMI's (1989a) first report on the implementation of the NC in primary schools. HMI found that 70 per cent of teaching time for children in year 1 was being spent on the core subjects although few classes taught the core subjects entirely separately. HMI concluded that 'Many schools are not well prepared to meet the reasonable time requirements, especially in areas such as technology, history or geography' (HMI 1989a: para. 48). The emphasis on core subjects in the schools surveyed in Summer 1989 may reflect the fact that the first NC subject documents to be published focused on these subjects. These documents were followed by the technology interim report in June 1989, by the history working party report in August 1989 and by other subject reports later. Even so, as history, geography, technology, and presumably PE, art and music were receiving insufficient time, one may be sceptical about whether activities outside the NC will have any chance of being developed.

RESPONDING TO PRESSURES OF TIME:

How can additional curricular work be fitted into the timetable on top of all of the foundation subjects and RE?

It might be said that it is all very well to talk about not being constrained by the NC and about going beyond it. This would work well enough if there were unlimited time available. However, the school day is short. One study of ILEA junior schools (Mortimore *et al.* 1988) found that the average teaching time in a day (i.e. excluding playtimes, dinner times, assembly, etc.) was approximately five hours. Even within this 'teaching day', time available for learning is curtailed. Barbara Tizard and her team (1988) found that non-work activities within the infant classroom (such as wandering about, tidying up, going to the lavatories, and registration) took up 17 per cent of children's time in the school day. There are two ways of increasing learning time in schools: to 'add time' and to use available time more effectively. In addition, in the context of the NC, there are various ways, such as 'double-counting' subject time, to increase time available for non-NC work.

Increasing the time available for teaching/learning

The ILEA junior school study (Mortimore *et al.* 1988) showed the diversity in time in school between different schools. Some children had a school day which was regularly forty minutes longer than that of other children. Over several school years such a difference would accumulate into a substantial difference in total time in school. Schools with a short day could consider ways of extending the day, perhaps by being more flexible about when children come into school. Do children have to wait outside (possibly in the cold) or, if a teacher is present, can they go into the classroom and start on activities? Many schools now have a much more flexible start to the school day in order to capitalise on children's enthusiasm for learning. The introduction of different patterns to the school day (the 'continental' day) or term (a four- rather than a three-term school year) may also use learning time better than more traditional patterns.

Ways of creating additional teaching/learning time include being more flexible about mid-morning, mid-afternoon and lunch time breaks. There may be ways of allowing children to carry on working over these times and taking shorter breaks if they choose to do so. This might entail having a rota of supervisors in the playground over, say, thirty minutes, and doubling up class supervision for short periods. Alternatively, breaks could be used more constructively, not just for children to 'let off steam' but as a time during which children play at various number or language games in a semi-structured way. In one London school in which I taught, the head regularly used 'wet' playtimes as a period when she took the whole school and taught them traditional London street rhymes and singing games. By the time the children left the school they had a large store of these which they shared with friends from other schools, taught to (or reminded) parents and older relatives and spontaneously sang and played in the playground and streets.

Simple marking out of the playground in a variety of ways (e.g. hopscotch, overlapping circles, dartboard patterns) can foster better use of this facility. Interestingly, the New Zealand Government produces a comprehensive handbook of playground ideas, which is distributed to all primary school teachers. This is an idea which could be copied in Britain and would perhaps be received more enthusiastically than some of the NC documents! Similarly, if the playground is turned into a more interesting environment then it can become a rich source for learning. Some schools have made imaginative conversions of their playgrounds from bald asphalt to multi-sensory wildlife environments in which different types of garden are developed in different areas of the playground. In such a school much environmental education can take place during playtimes! Peter Blatchford (1989) describes a wonderful example of such a school in Berkshire. I know also of schools in 'deprived' inner city areas in which similar conversions have been made, sometimes in the face of opponents who have feared that the attractive school environment would be rapidly vandalised. However, these fears have proved unjustified.

At present a major cause, in some areas, of children losing time in school is the shortage of teachers and it is perhaps ironic that, as some teacher unions have warned, the NC may be thwarted by this shortage. It is beyond the scope of this book to pursue this issue but it is clearly relevant. Strategies to add half an hour of learning time to a school day are immaterial if children are routinely sent home for half or whole days owing to teacher shortages.

Using classroom learning time more effectively

A second way of making more time for learning is by using time-tabled learning time more effectively; for example, by keeping routine administrative tasks to a minimum. The register could be completed by noting informally which children are present/ absent rather than making all children stop their activities to listen to the register. Similarly, if children are tuned into regular routines (such as knowing the time at which assembly takes place), they will get into the habit of stopping activities just before this time. Other strategies to use classroom learning time effectively are discussed in chapters 7 and 8.

One of the biggest challenges for the teacher of a child who has difficulties in school-based learning is to sustain the child's confidence and enthusiasm in learning. The greatest disincentive in learning anything is to experience repeated failure. Even adults, who should be relatively confident and mature, tend to react to failure by wanting to avoid the activity which prompted the failure. As a worker involved in an adult literacy scheme, I met many adults who had gone to great lengths to hide their inabilities to read or write competently, rather than try again to learn these skills. One woman was an Avon cosmetics representative who managed the whole process of taking and sending in orders by pointing to pictures and copying numbers from one form to another. When she explained to me how she sent in and then checked the orders it was clear that she had developed strategies which worked and avoided any 'reading'. It was her inability to read stories to her daughter which had prompted her long delayed, and ultimately successful, attempt at learning to read. Similarly, one man who had minimal reading skills ran a large and successful business. He said that no-one at his business knew of his poor reading because he dictated everything to his secretary and she read important in-coming mail on to a dictaphone machine.

Many teachers can recount the variety of minor ways in which some children will try to avoid a particular task. Sometimes this avoidance stems from failure and fear of failing again. Sharpening pencils, cleaning out the hamster's cage, sorting the book area, taking a note round to other classes or dinner numbers to the secretary, all seem to be well-tried ploys. Few children go to the lengths of one child I knew (a 9-year old boy) who ate the school goldfish rather than attempt, yet again, an activity which he found difficult. Such behaviour prompts questions about the actions of the teacher as well as of the child.

Children with learning difficulties do often avoid learning activities in schools. Diana Moses (1982), in an interesting study of junior school classes, found that although teachers spent more time with 'slow learners' than they did with 'average' children, the 'slow learners' were engaged in work or 'partial work' for just over half the time whereas 'average' children worked for nearly 70 per cent of the time. A range of research has shown that 'time on task' is closely correlated with attainment and, although one should be wary of making simplistic judgements about time on task (e.g. children staring vacantly into space may be thinking through a problem), it seems that a crucial issue for class teachers is how to find ways of maximising learning time and encouraging children with learning difficulties to carry on with learning activities.

Defining time allocations in the NC

In the context of the NC there may be scope for teaching material outside the foundation subjects by a 'double-counting' of the time spent teaching particular foundation subjects. For example, a discussion about a plant growing in the classroom could fulfil several parts of different POSs (e.g. English, science, geography and mathematics). Circular 6 (NCC 1989b) makes explicit reference to 'sharing attainment targets' (para. 12) so that, for example, oracy is developed across subject areas. The paragraph is written from the perspective of a secondary school ('The English teacher ... the mathematics teacher') but in the primary context it can be seen as a recognition that some ATs will be developed through several 'subjects'.

There is clearly a problem about fitting in all of the subject-based work, without adding the claims of cross-curricular and non-NC activities and yet, as discussed above, there is a strong case for these things. At the start of this chapter I quoted the NCC's (1990a) Curriculum Guidance 3 which stated clearly that the basic curriculum should not be the whole curriculum. It is important to hold on to this if curricula in schools are to be broadened, not narrowed, by the ERA. Chapter 3 considers some practical implications of working towards a curriculum which has breadth in several ways.

Chapter 3

Planning for a broad curriculum

Worries about the NC narrowing learning opportunities, especially for children with difficulties in learning, have prompted teachers to look imaginatively at ways of countering such narrowing. Two aspects of curricular breadth will be considered here: broad frameworks for the planning of teaching/learning, and strategies to promote later, as well as initial, stages of learning. Topic-based approaches will be discussed as a specific way of promoting various stages of learning.

FRAMEWORKS FOR PLANNING TEACHING

There have been three different frameworks put forward as ways of planning for a broad curriculum within the demands of the NC and the ERA. All of these frameworks apply to whole class planning, including work with children who find learning difficult.

Starting from NC subjects and cross-curricular themes

The most conventional solution is to list the foundation subjects, RE and cross-curricular themes and to plan work to cover all of these areas. This is likely to go some way towards meeting administrative demands to be seen to be teaching the NC but, for some teachers, it seems to be too focused on subject rather than on child.

Starting from cross-curricular strategies

A second approach is to start with the cross-curricular strategies, rather than subject-based documentation, and to plan the curriculum around the cross-curricular strategies. This is a response which is taken by some special schools and has intuitive appeal for many primary teachers. In this approach a school might begin by listing cross-curricular dimensions, leading to a policy statement of school principles in relation to issues such as equal opportunities. Then the school might look at cross-curricular themes (not only the NCC's 'pre-eminent' five) and map how these will be taught across and within classes. Next, cross-curricular skills are reviewed to check that these are being developed with continuity and progression. These three sets of cross-curricular strategies lead to reference to subject documentation. Thus, at the planning stage, the processes of learning and, in particular, the development of personal and social skills come before subject-centred knowledge. I can envisage this approach being very successful for children with severe learning difficulties for whom subject-centred learning may involve only the first few levels of statements of attainment (SOAs). It is more difficult (although possible) to translate the approach into contexts in which children will be acquiring a wide range of subject-specific knowledge, concepts and skills.

Starting from areas of learning and experience

The third way of planning for curricular breadth is to take an alternative framework from that of the NC. One such framework is that provided by HMI (DES 1985), in which nine areas of learning and experience were outlined:

- Aesthetic and creative
- Human and social
- Linguistic and literary
- Mathematical
- Moral
- Physical
- Scientific
- Spiritual
- Technological

These have been widely quoted and some authorities, notably Leicestershire in their key stages materials (Leicester LEA 1989), have developed ways of cross-referencing ATs with these areas of learning and experience. The appeal of this approach is that it retains an overall breadth (explicitly including human, social, spiritual and moral aspects of education) as well as approaching subject-based work from a wide disciplinary base (e.g. aesthetic, scientific and physical areas). The validity of these areas has been debated but they have much in common with theoretical models such as the forms of knowledge proposed by Paul Hirst (1974).

CURRICULAR BREADTH: PLANNING FOR VARIOUS STAGES OF LEARNING AND TEACHING

Several psychologists (e.g. Haring et al. 1978) have identified various stages in learning and have emphasised that the acquisition of skills or knowledge is only the first step in learning, not the whole process. This can be illustrated by the example of learning to drive a car. Initially, the learner driver probably learns how to drive a particular vehicle, and is hesitant and cautious, moving jerkily at first (the *acquisition stage* of learning). With time, the learner driver becomes more smooth and less jerky (the *fluency stage*). Then, with more time and practice, the learner driver is able to drive different makes and models of car (the *generalisation stage*) and to cope with driving with a broken arm or driving on the continent (the *adaptation stage*). Some people seem to go through these stages very rapidly and the four stages merge into one another as the learning takes place easily. For others, the process is long, slow and painful, with each stage having to be learned carefully and earlier steps having to be repeated and practised many times.

Teaching tends to focus on children's initial acquisition of knowledge and skills while relatively little attention is given to helping children to become fluent in these and in applying them to new contexts. Discussions about a broad curriculum for children who have difficulties in retaining teaching must, therefore include opportunities for later as well as initial stages of learning.

Developing fluency

One argument is that a child will only retain skills, concepts and knowledge when he or she has reached a particular level of fluency, that is, when the child can recall the information very rapidly. Most children reach this level quickly and easily but, for some, this is a long process which needs to be taught directly, just as some learner drivers have repeatedly to practise explicitly certain procedures (e.g. looking into the mirror before moving off) before this becomes automatic (fluent).

Techniques to develop fluency have been suggested by various writers. These techniques include games and approaches such as precision teaching which involve brief, timed, mini-tests of learning a specific skill. For example, a child who can recall multiplication facts but is not quick in doing so, might play various Snap-like games in order to speed up. An adult might give the child a short (perhaps only one-minute) test each day, which is presented as a game rather than as a formal test. The results from these mini-tests build up into a daily, then weekly, record of the number of multiplication facts recalled in each one-minute session. As the child's fluency improves, results can be shown on a graph and this is encouraging to the child as he or she can see that progress is being made. If progress stops or slows then the adult needs to simplify the test. (See Haring *et al.* 1978, Levey and Branwhite 1987, and Solity and Bull 1987 for discussion and examples of precision teaching techniques.) Simplified versions of this approach might involve a regular game in which the child works with an adult on a timed activity linked with the skill in which fluency is to be developed. Quick (timed) reading of a group of sight vocabulary words on small flashcards is one popular example.

Two important points from this work are that teachers need to have:

• A way of checking, and recording, whether or not earlier knowledge and skills have been retained,
• Strategies which are part of usual classroom activities and can be used to help children with learning difficulties to 'over-learn' skills and knowledge.

Using 'spare time'

Some teachers have systems of 'spare time' activities which they use for children with learning difficulties to practise, using material which has been learned (i.e. acquired). This might be organised by having a convention or classroom rule about what children do in 'spare time', and some teachers display this timetable in the classroom. Such a 'spare time' activities timetable could be devised for individuals or groups. Table 3.1 is an example of how a teacher might plan 'spare time' activities for several year 3 children with reading difficulties.

Table 3.1 Spare time activities: sample timetable

	For Julie and Mark	For Lucy and Sally
MONDAY	Micro-computer game	Taped sounds quiz
TUESDAY	Taped sounds quiz	Words quiz (on LM*)
WEDNESDAY	Letter sounds games	Own choice
THURSDAY	Words quiz (on LM*)	Micro-computer game
FRIDAY	Own choice	Letter sounds games

*LM = *Language Master* machine

Speed games

Various 'speed' games can be developed in the classroom to encourage children with learning difficulties to keep practising and rehearsing skills and knowledge until they reach a level at which these are retained over the longer term. These speed games might involve children timing one another against a clock (e.g. when rehearsing sight vocabulary words or number bonds). Clearly they need to be used sensitively so that they foster, not hinder, children's learning. If the atmosphere of the game becomes too tense and competitive, it is likely to be counter-productive. Often parental help at home can be used to develop children's fluency. For example, in some LEAs parents of children with moderate learning difficulties have been taught to use precision teaching techniques with their children. One advantage of such an approach is that the parents as well as the child can see that the child is maintaining skills. This kind of 'game' works best for relatively simple skills and should go alongside broader approaches to developing the child's learning. Similarly, some micro-computer software programs can help children to rehearse specific skills or to apply knowledge in an interesting way. These programs can often be personalised and immediate positive feedback included (e.g. smiley faces). The endless patience and unlimited questions from a micro-computer can, within limits, provide the sort of extensive practice which may otherwise not be found within usual class activities. If such practice is tied to a game format, then an individual child may obtain practice without this becoming tedious.

Maintaining fluency in skills and knowledge is not specific to the NC but its importance means that record sheets for children with learning difficulties should include both notes about fluency and regular checks to see that knowledge and skills have been retained. Teachers are likely to be particularly aware of this at the reporting ages, usually years 2 and 6, when continuous teacher assessments will be combined with SATs for reporting. The importance, for children with learning difficulties, of 'over-learning' knowledge and skills is illustrated in the following example.

An example: Wesley

Wesley was a 9-year old who could write a couple of short sentences but seemed unable to progress to writing stories or accounts without a great deal of help from the teacher. After talking through attempts at writing with Wesley, his teacher decided that the underlying difficulty was that Wesley, although he wanted to write, was unable to look up words quickly in a simple dictionary. Since she discouraged children from 'queueing' for words from her, and Wesley disliked asking other children for help, he had got into the habit of not writing very much in order to avoid the problem of going through, for him, a laborious process in order to locate the required word. Given time and structured help, Wesley could find words in the dictionary but he could not do this quickly on his own.

The teacher was involved in staff discussions to analyse the intermediate goals involved in being able to use a simple diction ry (discussed in Lewis 1985). From this, a range of games was devised to help children to over-learn alphabetical order. Wesley enjoyed these games and often chose to do them (e.g. during 'wet' playtimes). He became more confident about finding words on his own. The games were only one element of classroom activities designed to foster dictionary use. They did seem to help Wesley to make the transition from faltering and cautious use of his own word book (containing words written by the teacher) to a wider and effective use of various classroom word books, lists and dictionaries.

Providing children with opportunities to generalise and adapt knowledge, concepts and skills

An important aspect of developing learning for children with difficulties is ensuring that those children have opportunities to use knowledge and skills in new contexts. Being able to add up numbers is of limited use if this can only be done using a particular set of blocks; the ability to read certain words is of restricted use if those words are only recognised in one context (e.g. in a specific reading book). Topic-based approaches to the curriculum can be used to help children to apply knowledge, concepts and skills. A child who can add numbers up to 100 can be helped to generalise and adapt this ability by using it, for example, when devising a board game in which players add numbers on a modified die (its sides labelled, say, 32, 17, 23, etc.), or when making a model involving, say, finding two pieces of balsa wood to glue together to make a plane wing of 300 mm in length.

Some children find it hard to adapt or apply knowledge to new situations. For example, some children do not realise, unless it is explicitly pointed out, that the following require the same piece of mathematical knowledge:

(*spoken*)
- Two and five makes ...
- Two plus five equals ...
- A 2p coin and a 5p coin make ...
- A 2 m piece of wood added to a 5 m piece of wood gives me a piece of wood ... m long.

(*written*)
- $2 + 5 =$
- $5 + 2 =$
- $(2,5) \rightarrow$
- 2 +
  5
  —
  —
- 5 +
  2
  —
  —
- 2p + 5p =
- 2 Kg + 5 Kg =

Similarly, different print or handwriting styles
(e.g. A, a, α, Œ, 𝒜, and 𝒜) may not be interpreted as representing the same letter.

In the same way, a child with difficulties in learning may
understand that his or her runner bean needs water to grow.
However, if the child is then asked about what a lemon pip or an
oak tree needs to grow, or if the question is turned round and the
child is asked, 'If we stop watering the bean what will happen?',
then the child may be confused and unable to answer. These
questions require the child not just to understand the one instance
but also to be able to extrapolate the general rule and apply it to
relevant situations. It is at this point that learning may stop,
perhaps because the teacher has assumed that the child, having
understood the first instance, will have made the connection with
an understanding of the general rule. Consequently teaching
plans for children who have difficulties in learning need to include
the developing of generalisation and the adaptation of skills and
knowledge. This has always been an important, although sometimes overlooked, aspect of children's learning. Its importance has
been highlighted by the content of the NC foundation subjects,
many of which refer to children's abilities to adapt what is known
to a new situation. For example, the POS for technology, level 2,
states that pupils should be taught to make a simple appraisal of
products. This presumably means that the children should be able
to appraise a variety of products (e.g. toys, buildings, clothes), not
specific items only.

The SATs and other assessments at the reporting ages may
probe the child's ability to apply skills and knowledge. The following example, from a series of assessment tasks for 7-year olds
(Jones *et al.* 1989), illustrates the confusion which might arise for
a child with difficulties when given a simple but 'disguised' task:

Stripey and Curly go on a picnic with 2 friends, Flip and Flop.

(a) The 4 friends take 2 sandwiches each.
How many sandwiches are there altogether?

(b) They share a bag of 20 sweets between them and
have the same number of sweets each.
How many sweets do they each have?

(Activity booklet, *The Picnic*, p. 2–3)

Task (a) is asking: what is 4 x 2? A child with difficulties in mathematics might be able to do the multiplication but might not recognise that this is what is required in (a). Similarly (b) might not be recognised as asking: 20 divided by 4 = ?

This is an illustration of how a child who is competent on readily recognisable number tasks might appear to lack these skills because he or she fails to recognise the need to apply the particular skill(s). (Other issues concerning the assessment, using SATs, of children with learning difficulties are explored in chapter 10).

It is not being suggested here that teachers should have prescriptive lists of generalisation/adaptation activities through which children with learning difficulties work. Topic work can provide naturally many opportunities for children to practise skills and to demonstrate whether or not skills and knowledge can be generalised and applied. This is illustrated in the following example of one child's difficulties.

An example: Kate

Kate was an 8-year old with difficulties in reading. She had a small sight vocabulary but this was limited to recognising the words in her home-made reading book. She read fluently the whole sentences in the book and the individual words when these were shown separately, using *Breakthrough* sentence makers. Kate wanted a second reading book but her teacher was hesitant about going on as Kate was unable to recognise the words from her first book when they appeared elsewhere, such as in classroom notices. Kate seemed to have acquired an initial level of skill and was fluent in this fairly limited area, but could not generalise it to other contexts.

Kate enjoyed activities using machines, so the teacher made *Language Master* cards of the individual words from Kate's book. At about this time, Kate's mother had another baby and Kate was keen to draw and talk about this. The teacher encouraged Kate to make a 'baby book' containing a great variety of relevant pictures and information. This was not specifically a reading book but Kate, while making the baby book, independently copied relevant words from her first reading book on to appropriate pages of her baby book. She had used the *Language Master* cards to check that these were the words she wanted. She had pasted into the book some

Christening cards and it was these that seemed to help Kate to recognise that 'baby' could be written in various colours, scripts, etc. but still say 'baby'. The teacher believed that this was the first time that Kate had recognised for herself the generalisability of one of her sight vocabulary words. The teacher then made a class newspaper on which various items of news were written. Kate's baby news was included in this and from this point Kate began to recognise firstly her baby book words and then her reading book words in other contexts.

Motivational value of topic-based work

In chapter 2, issues to do with time spent learning and ways of maximising this were discussed. One way of utilising children's motivation for learning and of building on this is to encourage children to develop their own interests through topic- or project-based learning. Topic work, even when teacher-initiated, reflects a belief that children learn more effectively if subject-centred material is taught in a broader way, although individual topics may contain a bias towards a certain subject area (for example, a topic on wheels might have a science and technology bias but include art, poetry, drama, dance and history).

The extent to which a topic approach to developing learning is motivating for children may depend on how the topic is chosen. Ways of introducing topics range from wholly child-centred to more strongly teacher-initiated. At the child-centred end are situations in which learning develops naturally from a child's firsthand experiences (as when a child playing with junk modelling materials makes a model of a house and this is then developed with teacher guidance into an exploration of the properties of materials, stories about the people who live in the house, estimates of wallpaper to cover it, etc.). This approach requires much careful teacher guidance of children and direct teaching when the need for this is apparent. Its great strength is that it starts with the child's interests but difficulty arises in ensuring progression, balance and breadth in learning.

At the teacher-initiated end of the continuum are topics which are introduced by the teacher and which depend on his or her skill to make them link with the child's experiences. In teacher-initiated topic work, the topics are often planned through the school as a whole with particular topics (usually history, geography and science/technology) being allocated to specific years and terms. The last terms in years 2 and 6 are often left 'open' for work associated with SATs. The selection of the topics reflects a search for a way of encompassing work which is required in at least several of the foundation subjects without timetabling rigid slots for each of the ten subjects in the basic curriculum. Children with learning difficulties should be included in the class topic and chapter 6 includes examples of how work in two topics could be developed concurrently by children of different attainments.

An advantage of such planning of a series of topics is that it tries to ensure, at least at the planning stage, systematic coverage of NC POSs. A disadvantage is that it diminishes teachers' scope for developing topics spontaneously as they arise from children's interests. It may be that, for some primary school teachers, this type of pre-planning becomes an interim stage and that, when this approach has operated for a few years, teachers become so familiar with the content of NC POSs that they can shape individual children's topic work to encompass relevant material.

Both this and the preceding chapters have reviewed issues and practice concerning breadth in the curriculum. The following chapter examines one of the fundamental topics in all teaching but one which is of especial importance if children have difficulties in learning, that of identifying 'where children are at' in their learning.

Chapter 4

Identifying the point reached by the child

It is a truism that learning must start from the point at which the child is; how could it be otherwise? What is harder to achieve in practice is that teaching begins from where the child is or, to put it another way, that teaching matches the child's learning needs. The NC can be seen as one way of fostering this matching of child and curriculum. The SEAC documentation on teacher assessment (SEAC 1990a) emphasises the links between teaching, learning and assessment.

If a child (or adult) has difficulty in learning something then the reaction of anyone inclined to take on the role of teacher is invariably to try to find out exactly what the learner can and cannot do. For example, someone trying to teach a friend (who has repeatedly failed the driving test) to drive, might well start by guessing the approximate level of the friend's driving ability and then asking the friend to perform certain manoeuvres (e.g. reversing, doing a three-point turn, making a hill start, negotiating a multi-storey car park). As a result of watching the attempts at these exercises, the teacher will note perhaps that gear changing is still awkward, so that more complex tasks are still inappropriate. Alternatively, it may be clear that the learner is over-confident and, given some slowing down, could complete the manoeuvres success-fully. This example highlights a strategy which teachers in schools use, almost intuitively, when working with children with learning difficulties.

This strategy is the assessment of the learner through careful observation while he or she is engaged in attempts at the activity. It should be the starting point for all teaching but is sometimes lost as children are pushed on to the escalators of published schemes and swept along! Also, in a busy classroom, it is all too easy for

continuous assessments of how children are learning to be replaced by quick assessments of the end-products.

An appropriate starting point for both further learning and the
teacher's teaching is crucial for children (and adults) who find
something difficult to learn. Most adults can recall something
which they have found hard to 'pick up'; for example, learning to
speak a foreign language, to play a musical instrument or to use a
word processor. Sometimes difficulties can be traced to a teacher
who 'started at the wrong place', assuming too much of the novice
learner.

This section will consider ways in which the teacher might
identify appropriate starting points in learning/teaching for
children who are finding tasks difficult. Advice and information
from other teachers and the child's care-givers, in addition to
careful observation of the child, can help to identify 'where the
child is'. This is particularly important for children starting
compulsory schooling, as the diversity of pre-infant school
provision means that the reception class is likely to include 5-year
olds with widely different experiences and expectations about
school (this is discussed more fully in David and Lewis 1991). In a
recent discussion that I had with a group of primary teachers, they
identifed fourteen different types of pre-school settings from
which reception class children may have come (including infant
school class, nursery unit, nursery class, nursery school, playgroup,
childminder, workplace crèche, family centre and home).

The diversity of pre-infant school experiences, and how the
reception class teacher might build on these, raises issues about
'baseline' assessment of children at the start of key stage 1 (Tizard
1988, Nuttall and Goldstein 1989, Thomas 1989). The term
'baseline' assessment has been used to refer to assessment near to
the start of full-time compulsory schooling. It has misleading con-
notations of children coming into reception classes with minimal
educational attainments, whereas a wide variety of research (e.g.
Tizard *et al.* 1988) has shown the richness of experiences and
attainments which children have on starting formal schooling.

Those in favour of assessing children at school entry on NC-
related targets argue that this provides a measure against which to
assess children's attainments at age 7. This argument draws heavily
on marketing notions of 'value added' to a product. It is said that
assessments of value-added would distinguish between a school
which has initially high-attaining pupils who nevertheless make

relatively little further progress over the next few years in school and a school which receives a relatively low-attaining intake but makes great progress with the children. The latter school may, in terms only of reported attainments at age 7, appear to be less successful than the former 'high intake' school. It has also been argued that including NC assessments on school entry provides a sound and sensible base from which to monitor children's progress on the NC. This is seen as important because of the diversity of children's pre-school experiences.

However, those who are against baseline assessments at age 5, in relation to the NC, maintain that this will label some children as 'failures' from their first days in school. It is also said that assessment results will eventually be linked in an undesirable way with teacher appraisal, reflecting a return to a covert payment by results system. More fundamentally, some of those who have argued against NC-linked assessment on school entry hold that this would be contrary to the basic principles of early childhood education (e.g. Bruce 1987), which emphasise acceptance of children's individuality and an avoidance of crude assessments of children's abilities in terms of products of learning. Linked with these two last points is the argument that such young children cannot be assessed in these terms in ways which are valid and reliable.

These divergent views reflect contrasting ideas about the purposes of this 'baseline' assessment. The 'value-added' arguments imply a prime concern with accountability: attainments at age 5 are only made in order to provide a comparison with attainments at age 7. A second purpose, in the special needs context, and one which was advocated in the 1970s, was assessment at age 5 in order to identify children thought likely to have later difficulties in learning. This psychological orientation hinged on the predictive validity of the tests used and is still being debated. It was argued that if it can be 'proved' that, for example, not being able to read letter sounds at age 5 predicts being a poor reader at age 7, then all children should be tested on letter sound knowledge at age 5. In practice, if teachers think that a child will find reading difficult, then they try to prevent this! Consequently, attempts to use attainments at age 5 predictively have often been confounded (rightly) by practice. For most teachers, the purpose of assessment, interpreted broadly, of children starting school is to make teaching more effective by getting to know a whole range of things about each child and where he or she is in his or her learning. Increasingly, information from parents and care-givers is integrated into the school's formal (Wolfendale 1989) and informal (David and Lewis 1991) assessment procedures.

What I am advocating in this chapter is careful assessment, through various forms of observation (not formal tests) of the point reached by a child in his or her learning, and teaching which builds on this knowledge. It is not being suggested that starting points for, say, 5-year olds should be only in terms specifically and directly linked with NC ATs. Broader assessment based on observation is important for all children but particularly for any children thought to have difficulties in learning.

ASSESSMENT OF 'ACTUAL' OR 'POTENTIAL' LEARNING?

Learning potential has been a very seductive topic in education and among its victims are the writers of some of the NC circulars. For example, Circulars 6/89 and 2/90 (DES 1989b, 1990b) contain an identical paragraph stating that: 'Schools should bear in mind that the objective of the National Curriculum is to ensure that each pupil should obtain maximum benefit, by stretching the pupil to reach his or her potential, but without making impossible demands' (paras 58 and 33 respectively). Similarly, Circular 22/89 (DES 1989c) refers to 'cultural differences' masking the child's 'true learning potential' (para. 88). Both sets of statements are about not expecting too little of children. This is an important point but the argument is hampered by referring to 'potential' as if children are recalcitrant elastic bands. Assessments of 'potential' are impossible, as no one can *know* another's potential. All we can make are best guesses (as valid and reliable as possible) which give a partial view of some current attainments and attitudes.

OBSERVATION

Observation of children is a vital first step in planning how their learning can be fostered. Observation can take many forms, structured or unstructured, involving the teacher working with the child or remaining distanced. When and how teachers observe children will depend both on the aims of that observation and on what is realistically feasible within a busy classrooom. While teachers recognise that watching how children are learning is an important part of teaching (and this is a particularly strong tradition in the early years of schooling), it requires careful planning to incorporate such activity into normal classroom life.

Teachers may make time for observing children by doing more collaborative teaching in which one teacher takes main responsibility for two class groups while the other teacher observes/works closely with a small group. Similarly, other classroom adults can be utilised (e.g. student teachers) so that a class teacher has observation time. A variety of occasions arising unexpectedly (e.g. in the playground) may provide the opportunity for informal observational assessments. Adults, other than the teacher, might also carry out the observations if given clear and detailed training about how to do this. I have worked with nursery nurses in primary schools who, using structured observation schedules, have monitored the integration of children from special schools (discussed further later). Similar work is described in accounts of Sunnyside Primary School's experiences of integration (Bell and Colbeck 1989). This type of work can generate valuable data about whether or not children with difficulties in learning are isolated in mainstream school classes and about the types of activities in which they are engaged.

The following discussion considers various approaches to continuous teacher assessments of children's development and learning, from relatively informal approaches to more formal and child-specific methods. Although they are of general relevance, they are particularly important in the planning of teaching and learning for children with difficulties for whom classroom work often seems to be mis-matched.

General classroom observations

A variety of general observations helps the teacher to get to know individual children. For example:

- In which kinds of activity does the child concentrate better or less well? What are typical periods of concentration for the child on particular activities?
- Which kinds of activity seem to be most meaningful for the child?
- In which kinds of activity is the child most confident?

- Does the child have a preference for certain kinds of materials (e.g. micro-computer based or linked with a particular piece of equipment such as a synchrofax or *Language Master* machine)?
- Does the child work better at certain times of the day (e.g. always tired in the first part of the morning or regularly livelier after the midday break)?
- Are there particular classroom friends with whom the child works well or poorly?
- What motivates the child to learn?
- What special interests does the child have?
- In which kinds of classroom grouping does the child work better or less well?
- Does the child prefer a noisy or quiet working environment?
- How does the child respond if given scope for developing his or her own ideas?

All of these things relate to getting to know the child and, once identified, they can be built on positively so that the classroom fosters rather than hampers learning. In the longer term it would be important that children who favoured a particular learning style (e.g. using computer-based materials) had experience in using other approaches also.

The importance of motivation in influencing what children are apparently capable of is illustrated in the following account. A 7-year old, Sarah, seemed unable to write even a sentence towards a story or 'news'. However, one day Sarah received a party invitation from a friend, Marie, in another class. She took the invitation home and showed it to her father, who wrote a reply saying that Sarah could come to the party. Sarah lost this note on her way to school the next day and became very upset about this. Her class teacher reassured her, saying that it would be all right as she would pass on the message to Marie's teacher for her to give to Marie. However, later that day Sarah handed her teacher a carefully written note saying: 'To Marie, I am coming to your party. From Sarah.' Sarah had written the note and may have had help from other children with spellings but, highly anxious not to miss the party, she had been prompted to write a message. The message had a real purpose and brought out her writing abilities.

A class teacher probably cannot individualise learning to such an extent that, even if he or she knows how every child responds to the features listed above, the class can be organised on this basis.

However, knowing how children respond to different situations and discussing this with the children's care-givers will help the teacher to make informed decisions about classroom organisation. These general observations may alert the teacher to possible hearing or visual impairments in a child.

Observation as a guide to sensory impairments

Sensory impairments, perhaps mild or transitory, may underlie or compound difficulties in learning. If a child cannot see his or her work clearly or cannot hear instructions clearly then it is likely that what the child does will appear to be 'wrong'. There is a wide range of cues which might convey to an observer that the child has hearing difficulties. These include the child:

- Appearing to ignore the teacher's questions,
- Having a frequent lack of attention in oral activities,
- Having difficulty in following directions,
- Depending on classmates for instructions,
- Tilting his or her head at an angle to hear a sound,
- Having speech difficulties,
- Having frequent ear infections,
- Sitting close to the TV or radio,
- Doing badly on auditory discrimination games such as identifying rhyming words,
- Having discharges from the ear(s),
- Talking with a very loud voice.

It has been estimated that approximately one in every ten young children has some hearing impairment, so it is possible, especially at the infant school stage, that learning difficulties will be related to hearing difficulty. If a teacher suspects that a child does have a hearing impairment then formal audiometric testing can be requested. An interim stage might be to give the child a simple individual hearing test requiring the child to identify a particular picture from a group of pictures with similar sounding names (e.g. cap, fan, cat, lamb). The Royal National Institute for the Deaf (RNID) has produced spiral-bound books of relevant pictures, carefully selected so that consistent errors will highlight particular types of hearing difficulty; for example, those concerning low frequency sounds (RNID 1970).

Similarly, the observant teacher can pick up a number of cues indicating visual difficulties in a child. These cues include the child:

- Complaining of aches in the eye(s) especially after long periods of close work,
- Rubbing his or her eyes vigorously,
- Closing or covering one eye,
- Showing sensitivity to light,
- Complaining about reflections from whiteboards or black-boards,
- Holding reading materials very near or far from the eyes,
- Sitting close to the TV/computer screen,
- Squinting or frowning when doing close work,
- Complaining of blurred vision,
- Confusing letters/numerals of similar shape,
- Having recurrent inflammation of the eyes,
- Having poor handwriting,
- Finding difficult a variety of fine hand–eye co-ordination tasks.

Colour blindness can easily pass unnoticed. One teacher I met told me of how her son, after a successful and happy few years in an infant school, had many problems on transferring to the junior school. It emerged that the junior school, unlike the infant school, used green chalkboards and her son could not distinguish clearly between the board writing and the green background. This had led him to avoid class work and to make many errors when he did attempt it. Neither she nor the previous school had suspected that her son was colour blind, although subsequent tests showed that he had red–green colour blindness, hence the particular problems with green chalkboards. Presumably such children would have similar difficulties with certain combinations of worksheet/workcard and ink colours. If visual difficulties are suspected then formal eye testing can be requested.

Further information about identifying and responding to sensory difficulties can be found in SNAP (Ainscow and Muncey 1984) and TIPS (Dawson 1985) materials. The RNID and RNIB, as well as other charitable foundations (see Male and Thompson 1985), will also give advice.

If hearing and/or visual difficulties are suspected then liaison with care-givers about the issue is very important. It is worth noting that a history of hearing or visual difficulties at the pre-infant school stage might be reflected in poor language or graphic skills in the infant school. Pre-infant school records and discussions with care-givers help to identify earlier difficulties. Of course, the presence of sensory impairments does not necessarily mean that the child will have (or have had) difficulties in learning.

Systematic observation

It may be appropriate to carry out some systematic observations of children, using structured observation schedules. These involve recording children's activities, using a schedule based on pre-specified lists or categories of observed behaviours, often monitored over regular time periods (e.g. every 30 seconds). The use of these schedules was briefly referred to earlier in relation to using different adults to make classroom observations. Systematic schedules are particularly useful for monitoring social behaviour. They can also be useful when monitoring a group of children in order to ascertain, for example, which children in the group contribute most to the conversation.

The following approach (adapted from Sylva *et al.* 1980) was used by staff in several schools who were monitoring the kinds of classroom interaction in which children with severe learning difficulties in primary schools were involved. The approach could be adapted for a variety of situations and aims.

1 Decide which children you want to observe and why.
  Let other staff know who these children are and when you will be observing them.
  You might decide to focus on a small number of children, observing each child in turn.
2 Prepare a sheet on which to record your observations. Draw horizontal lines to demarcate each 1-minute time band.
3 Observe for several minutes before you start to make notes.
4 Observe each target child in turn for five minutes.
5 Write down: (a) What the child says (language),
                      (b) With whom the child interacts (social),
                      (c) What the child does (activity),
  This should be factual not interpretative.
  Do this for each 1-minute band.
6 Afterwards, code each of the three sections. The codings will be specific to the context but might include:

    (a) REQ request
           PS   personal statement
    (b) SOL solitary
          INA interacting with adult
          INC interacting with another child
    (c) TT   teaching a task to another child

7 The results could then be put on to a graph or chart to show, for example, the proportion of time that the child(ren) is/are involved in solitary activities.

8 If possible, have two adults make observations simultaneously on the same child(ren). This will help to show whether or not the observations are reliable.

9 Consider the implications, for classroom practice, of what has been observed.

10 Consider repeating the observation exercise, with any necessary amendments to the original schedule.

There are both strengths and disadvantages in using structured, systematic observation schedules within a classroom. If the schedule is clearly structured and appropriate for the aims then it can supply useful information. It can show whether or not a teacher's impression is justified, for example, that a particular child habitually concentrates much better on oral than on written activities, or that two children work more productively together than separately. However, a structured observation schedule may be difficult to use effectively. Children may interrupt or behave differently because they are aware of being monitored. The use of structured observation schedules also requires at least two adults to be present, one to carry out the observations and one to work with the class. Several detailed accounts of formal observational methods (e.g. Croll 1986, Slee 1987, Sylva and Neill 1990) expand on their use in classrooms.

Observational methods are useful ways in which teachers can build up judgements about individual children and the dynamics of the classroom. They may also point to features of the classroom which the teacher could improve, such as making certain types of resources more accessible (discussed in chapter 8) or changing the location of some materials so that withdrawn children become more involved with other children. So far in this chapter, identifying the point reached by a child has focused on observations of children's general development and behaviour. Observational methods need to be supplemented with assessments which focus on curricular tasks. The SEAC (1990a) materials on teacher assessment provide many pointers for ways in which this can be done across the ability range. The next part of this chapter considers curriculum-based assessment in relation to children with difficulties in learning.

CHILD–ADULT CONFERENCES

It is useful if the teacher can observe a child both working alone on a particular activity and working alongside the teacher. This is important because it enables the teacher to assess, first, the processes of learning and not just the end-products and, second, what the child can do alone compared with what he or she can do with some guidance. This kind of activity is described in the TGAT report (DES/WO 1988a) and in NC-linked assessment materials (SEAC 1990a).

I recently watched a 6-year old boy, Sanjit, carrying out some work on making a block graph to show the numbers of children in the class staying for school dinner, eating a packed lunch or going home. Sanjit moved around the classroom with a sheet of paper on which there were three columns, depicting each of these choices. Sanjit asked each child which category he or she was in and then that child placed a tick in the appropriate column. Sanjit transferred the information from the ticked columns to a sheet of squared paper to produce a block graph containing the three sets ('school dinners', 'packed lunch' and 'home'). Sanjit completed the first two bars correctly on his own and I thought that he had done this by counting the number of ticks in each column and then counting up the same number of squares to produce the bar. However, when I talked to Sanjit about drawing the third bar, it became clear that he was not counting the ticks to determine the length of the bar but was using one-to-one matching to produce bars of the correct height. These two strategies (one-to-one matching and counting) have different implications for helping Sanjit to make the next step in his understanding.

Similarly, a group of children working on addition of money could arrive at the correct answer in different ways. Asked to add 12p and 8p (whether in the context of playing in a class shop, using workcards or worksheets or playing a game), children could arrive at the correct answer by counting on in ones (with or without coins or other materials), adding 12 and 8 as 'wholes', or adding 10 and 5 and then adding the remaining 2 and 3 respectively to make 20 (with or without coins). The different strategies used would suggest different types of activity to foster the next step in their learning. These examples show that talking to a child about how a task has been carried out can be very important even if the child has arrived at an appropriate answer. It is more usual for teachers, who are inevitably very busy in the classroom, to carry out this interviewing process only when children have made obvious errors.

Several writers have drawn attention to the importance of teachers 'interviewing' children as they work, to monitor the children's learning strategies. It is important for all children but especially so for children who seem to have difficulty in learning. Various terms have been used for this type of activity, including 'TIC' (Teacher interaction with the child; Hunter-Carsch 1990), tutorial dialogue (Meadows and Cashdan 1988), 'analytical interviews' (Bennett *et al.* 1984) and diagnostic teaching (e.g. Stott 1978). I am using the term 'child–adult conferences' because this emphasises the two-way sharing of information focusing on a specific activity.

Evidence from HMI reports (e.g. DES 1978b, 1988a) and individual research projects suggest that this kind of activity is rarely found in primary schools. One study of 4-year olds in school noted:

> Diagnosis of children's understandings were very noticeable by their absence, or were limited to brief encounters of an unsatisfactory kind ... [Teachers] very rarely had to deem a task, or a child, a failure, since they were always able to find some aspect acceptable. It follows from this that almost every task could be judged a success, which is precisely what teachers did, irrespective of whether or not the child, or the work, had been seen.
>
> (Bennett and Kell 1989: 82)

This suggests that teachers do need to become more used to carrying out conferences with children to ascertain children's approaches to a task and whether or not learning towards specific goals is being promoted. Roger Beard (1987) suggests that it would be helpful for teachers to divert time from routinely hearing children read to carrying out less frequent, but more in-depth, reading interviews with children. The NC, with its emphasis on continuous teacher assessments, will require the kind of approach advocated by Roger Beard and others. Child–adult conferences are discussed here because they are central to identifying the points in learning that are reached by individual children.

The various approaches to child–adult conferencing give several pointers about how this may be done effectively in a primary school class.

Organisation

- Acknowledge that it will be done relatively infrequently but in some detail for individual children.
- Acknowledge that some children will need this more frequently than do other children.
- Discourage other children from interrupting the activity.
- Avoid handing over this task to other adults in the classroom unless they fully understand its purpose and how to carry it out.
- Making time for child-adult conferences will require that teachers make more use of techniques in which children work without direct teacher involvement (e.g. collaborative work with classmates and self-checking games).
- It may be useful to tape record the conference so that it can be analysed later. The tape will also provide evidence about the child's learning which could be kept as a record. Children often like to hear such tapes re-played and to comment on their learning and interaction with the teacher.
- Capitalise on occasions when the child is highly motivated and has a good relationship with the teacher, especially if this happens infrequently.

Key questions

- Can the child explain why he or she is carrying out an activity in a certain way?
- What can the child do alone, compared with prompting? This is also very important for identifying able children who are doing work well below that of which they are capable.
- What can the child do already on his or her own? (Teaching should extend not duplicate this.)

- Has the child retained earlier steps in learning? For example, a child who has difficulty in completing tens and units sums involving carrying might have forgotten the 'base 10' concept underlying the activity.
- Can the child complete a given task in one context and transfer it to another context (e.g. add numbers using beads on a string and using a number line)?
- Can the child apply knowledge and skills in a new context (e.g. multiply numbers in a maths game and use multiplication facts to work out the numbers of rulers needed by groups of children in an art activity)?
- Can the child respond to a variety of question types (e.g. questions requiring recall, evaluation, speculation, problem solving)? (For example, after a science activity: what happened when we ...? could it have been done in a better way ...? what might happen if we ...? how did you feel about ...?)
- Does the child understand what he or she is being asked to do? For example, does he or she understand the vocabulary of the teacher's question?

Will Swann (1988) gives a good example which illustrates this last point. He describes talking to a 5-year old girl during her first week at school. The girl was drawing around flat, plastic shapes. He asked her, in the course of the conversation, how many sides the square had and in response the girl laid out, side by side, three other squares. He put them back and asked the girl to show him a side of a square. She pointed to the centre of the top surface of one square. He goes on to discuss the various and ambiguous contexts in which the girl may have come across the word 'side' (sides of a team, sitting side by side, the side of a cupboard, etc.) and conjectures that the girl's responses reflected her thinking through different meanings of 'side'. He concludes that the child's 'difficulty' with the task was largely illusory and that the real problem was a failure of communication on his part, and not the child's.

The ambiguity of teachers' talk, particularly in the reception class, when children may not have become socialised into school procedures and expectations, has been documented by Shirley Cleave and co-workers (1982) and by Mary Willes (1983). Both sets of research provide salutory reading, as they indicate the potential for misunderstandings in classrooms. Examples include a child who interpreted the teacher's instruction, 'Would you like to join the story group now', as an invitation ('no thank you') and children being confused by the ambiguities of the teacher's request for them to 'line up'. Children who find school learning difficult may be slower than other children to tune into the specific language conventions of the classroom. This point is considered further in chapter 10 in connection with SATs.

Diagnostic assessment

There is a relatively strong tradition of child–adult conferences, in special needs contexts, for diagnostic purposes. This is illustrated in various approaches to assessing and helping children with reading difficulties. Child–adult conferences are widely supported in this context, although there are differing views about the best focus of the conference. Two contrasting foci have been strongly advocated. One focus, developed from formal testing of 'sub-skills', has been on the psychological sub-skills believed to underlie particular tasks, notably reading. Thus, for example, many 'reading readiness' tests have included assessments of the child's visual sequencing (e.g. identifying the next letter(s) in a regular sequence), auditory sequencing (e.g. recalling aural sequences of letters or numbers) and visual memory (e.g. drawing from memory a shape shown briefly). The rationale was that reading was composed of discrete and identifiable sub-skills which could be isolated and measured. It then seemed logical to identify and remedy, by specific teaching, any weak sub-skills. Unfortunately, there was generally little transfer from resultant proficiency in the sub-skill(s) to facility in reading. Many writers and researchers concerned with assessing dyslexia and other 'specific learning difficulties' argue that those specific difficulties support this approach (Snowling 1985, Heaton and Winterson 1986). This is still controversial, mainly because the implications of such diagnostic assessments for subsequent teaching of the child are unclear although some writers (e.g. Bryant and Bradley 1985) have gone some way towards making these links.

A different focus in child–adult conferences has been on analyses of children's errors in a particular activity. Systematic analyses of errors (or 'miscues') can provide useful clues for teaching. For example, there are different implications for teaching in the case of James, who repeatedly makes phonic errors in spellings (e.g. 'storiz' for 'stories'), compared with Toni, who fails to apply a common spelling rule (e.g. she writes 'storys' for 'stories', 'worrys' for 'worries', etc.). Miscue analyses have been discussed in detail in relation to spelling (Peters 1975), reading (Arnold 1982), handwriting (Alston and Taylor 1987) and mathematics (Hughes 1986). How the teacher analyses errors and chooses on which errors to focus will reflect his or her theories (possibly implicit) about the nature of the knowledge/skills and the processes of acquiring these.

Curriculum-based assessment: planning multi-level tasks/activities

The strongest type of assessment embodied in the NC is curriculum-based assessment. In the early stages of the introduction of the NC, continuous curriculum-based assessment will require that the teacher has a bank of activities which can be carried out at a variety of levels. This is a development of the kind of thing that teachers often do when working with a class or group of children for the first time. They might ask children to draw a picture and write a word, sentence or story to go with it. The level at which the child responds conveys information about the child's abilities in handwriting, story or report writing, creativity and pencil control as well as, possibly, aspects of the child's self-esteem and motivation. In time, multi-level tasks will be important for teaching (see chapter 6) but less crucial in terms of initial teacher assessments. The previous teacher(s) should have been maintaining good, NC-linked records of assessment from which other teachers can continue.

A teacher could assess children's starting points on the curriculum by using the broad type of activity suggested above. Another way is to work with a group of children carrying out the same activity but to vary the question level. Two examples are given here, the first relating to a science AT and the second to a geography target.

Science AT 10: Forces

Pupils should develop their knowledge and understanding of forces; their nature, significance and effects on the movement of objects.

(DES\WO 1989a: 22)

Play with sand could, through guided questioning by the teacher, probe several levels of this attainment target. For example:

- 'Can you send your truck over to mine?'
  (Level 1: knows that things can be moved by pushing them.)
- 'They're going to crash. How are you going to stop your truck from crashing?'
  (Level 2: understand that pushes and pulls can make things start moving, speed up, swerve or stop.)
- 'My truck's going up the sand bank. Why has it stopped now?'

  (Level 3: understand that when things are changed in shape, begin to move or stop moving, forces are acting on them.)

Geography AT 2: The home area and region

Pupils should develop their knowledge and understanding of the geography of the home area and region, leading to an appreciation of the local and regional 'sense of place'.

(DES\WO 1990a:21)

This also could be assessed at several different levels through one activity. Children could draw a picture (map) of their route from home to school. At the simplest level this could be very crude and show just one path between two buildings. Questioning could probe the level reached by the child:

- 'Where do you live?'
  (Level 1: demonstrate that pupils know their home address.)
- 'What do you pass on your way to school?'
  (Level 2: recognise different work and leisure activities, uses of land and buildings in the surrounding area.)
- 'Why is the supermarket on the main road?'
  (Level 3: offer simple explanations why some activities in their home area are located where they are.)
- 'Draw the roads going from the school to ... [nearby village/ town/city].'
  (Level 4: explore the links between their local area and other places in the home region.)

The information gained through these kinds of activities could be combined with information from the children's care-givers and previous teachers in order to clarify the current starting points for the children's learning.

This chapter has examined the importance of trying to identify where children are in their learning. Several possible foci, some ways of carrying out individual assessments and ways of incorporating these into classroom activities have been discussed. Identifying children's starting points is the first step in planning teaching. Curriculum-based assessment is, in the contexts of both the NC and past work in relation to children with difficulties in learning, part of a continuous cycle of teaching and assessment. For that reason, curriculum-based assessment is considered further in the following chapter.

Chapter 5

Helping children to gain access to the National Curriculum

Planning intermediate goals

Intermediate goals can be thought of in terms of the task (task analysis) or of the teacher's role. The more usual way of thinking about planning intermediate goals is the former: analysing the task or activity. Both of these are linked with sustaining progression and continuity in children's learning.

ANALYSING THE TASK AND THE TEACHER'S ROLE

Teachers work, usually implicitly, with models of broad sequences of learning. These underlie their choices, in a 'child-centred' classroom, about provision for children's opportunities for learning or, in a more 'teacher-centred' environment, about which learning tasks are presented to children. How these kinds of models or 'images' develop has been the focus of work on the development of teachers' professional knowledge (e.g. Elbaz 1983, Calderhead 1988).

It is important to work out what may be the components that are involved in acquiring a particular area of learning because, through these, the next steps in the child's learning can be identified. This is so whether the teacher supports a relatively child-centred or a subject-centred approach to fostering children's learning. In the former case, the identification of components or intermediate goals will lead the teacher to guide the child towards certain activities and to provide particular resources; in the latter case, teaching will be explicitly directed at the components (e.g. Reason and Boote 1986, Solity and Bull 1987). Similarly, different theoretical stances in special education, including behavioural (e.g. Ainscow and Tweddle 1979) and cognitive (Sugden 1989), advocate division of learning targets into possibly broad, but smaller, steps. This advocacy is continued in various NC documents. For example:

> In the process of giving pupils with s.e.n. the opportunity to demonstrate their level on the statements of attainment, teachers will often find it necessary to structure their schemes of work in such a way as to provide a series of intermediate goals, though it will be found that some attainment targets can be broken down more easily than others into smaller steps. In such circumstances teachers will want to adapt their existing record systems to bring them in line not only with the statements of attainment themselves but with the small steps leading to them.
>
> (NCC 1989d: 12)

Teacher observations of the child (discussed in chapter 4) will help the teacher to decide when, and in how much detail, activities need to be divided into smaller steps. The greater a child's difficulties in learning, the sharper will be the need for a focus on dividing activities into tentative 'intermediate goals'. The need, within the NC framework, to sub-divide elements of the POSs into smaller parts, especially those relevant to key stage 1, is apparent from various research evidence. Brian O'Toole and Pamela O'Toole (1989) have suggested that many 7-year olds with learning difficulties will not succeed in level 1 ATs (2–4) in number. They concluded that work needed to be done to break down NC tasks into small attainable steps. Similarly, but involving older children, Michael Shayer (1989) has speculated that, in relation to science, a substantial proportion of children at secondary school level will fall below the 'minimum' indicated in the TGAT Report (DES/WO 1988a) as the 'normal' ranges for key stages 3 and 4.

Both these studies suggest that there will be a longer 'tail' to the spread of attainments on NC ATs than was indicated in the TGAT Report. If this does turn out to be the case then it means that the distance between levels of SOAs will, for a number of children, be much longer than the nominal two years. Consequently, POSs intended to cover a two-year period will stretch over a far longer period for some children. This will require teachers to sub-divide the programmes of study more finely than may have been anticipated. A number of individuals, groups of teachers and educationalists have already begun to divide POSs for key stage 1 and early levels of ATs into broad components or associated activities (e.g. Archer 1989, EYCG 1989, Tilstone and Steel 1989). The professional associations such as NARE (National Association for Remedial Education), which have produced sub-divisions of pre-NC curricula (e.g. Herbert and Davies-Jones 1984, Turnbull 1981), may adapt these in the light of the NC.

Before going on to outline ways in which some parts of the NC POSs might be sub-divided, it is worth noting that there are some difficulties about this strategy in the context of the NC. One needs to be clear on which level the sub-division is to focus: SOA, AT or POS?

POSSIBLE DANGERS IN TRYING TO SUB-DIVIDE SOAs

Some commentators on the NC for children with SEN have advocated sub-dividing SOAs, the narrowest and most specific aspect of the NC. It has been argued that, in this way, the NC can be made to accommodate the learning needs of children with a wide range of difficulties, including children with multiple and profound learning difficulties. This approach works well for sequential and hierarchical skills, such as some aspects of number, and there is research support for the approach in that context (Cronbach and Snow 1977). However, attempts to produce definitive teaching or learning sequences for broader conceptual development have failed. Robert Gagné (1968), investigating this issue, emphasised the ability of a learner to skip sections, to draw on skills from other curricular or psychological areas, to use atypical combinations of sub-skills to arrive at a target and to achieve success by 'scrambled' sequences.

Analysing successive SOAs into series of small steps implies that the levels within ATs are logical and sequential. It treats SOAs as if they had a scientific precision, when they are indeed tentative, and as yet barely tested, guesses about sequences and levels of learning targets. Consequently, analysis of small steps between successive SOAs may run into problems of various sorts.

Sequence

I suspect that most teachers would agree that, at an intuitive level, it makes sense to teach a child addition to 10 and then addition to 100 (Mathematics AT 2, levels 1 and 2 respectively); it is less clear whether, for example, knowing that the weather has a powerful effect on people's lives will necessarily precede knowing that air is all around us (Science AT 9, SOAs levels 2 and 3 respectively).

Similarly, Science AT 9, earth and atmosphere, assumes that understanding and interpreting common meteorological symbols as used in the media (level 3) will come after recording the weather over a period of time in words, drawings, and charts (level 2). However, many children seem to recognise the pictographic weather symbols, which they often see on television, long before they can record the weather for themselves.

Interval

In addition to problems concerning sequence, some SOAs appear to place a very short gap in learning between two successive levels. This gap is nominally representative of two years' learning but in some cases this seems doubtful. For example, Technology AT 3 has almost identical SOAs at levels 1 and 2 ('use a variety of materials and equipment to make simple things' and 'show that they can use simple hand tools, materials and components', respectively). Whether or not this step is 'two years' learning will depend on what kinds of tools and materials are introduced at each stage. An identical activity, such as making a paper boat using scissors and a ruler, could be acceptable for both levels. The distance between these SOAs could be minimal, in which case it would be difficult to find reasonable ways of sub-dividing this into smaller steps. Attempts to sub-divide the small gap might lead to an unnecessary slowing down in learning pace.

Specificity

Some of the difficulties concerning interval reflect the vagueness of some SOAs, such as those just cited. Vagueness is associated particularly with level 1 SOAs and it could be argued that this will help to ensure that all children are perceived as having reached at least level 1. This is considered again in chapter 10 in discussion of SATs.

Progression

Progression within an attainment target is evident across the ten levels. However, in some cases, later SOAs do not clearly build on earlier ones but seem to introduce many new concepts. A division of, say, some level 3 SOAs will therefore entail an analysis of many areas, not just a bridge between levels 2 and 3. For example, Science AT 5, human influences on the earth, gives the following SOAs at level 3: pupils should (i) know that human activity may produce local changes in the Earth's surface, air and water; and (ii) be able to give an account of a project to help to improve the local environment. At the next level (level 4), one SOA is given: pupils should know that some waste materials can be recycled. A reasonable sub-division of this level 4 SOA into small steps might be quite independent of the two level 3 SOAs (e.g. it could include: identifying waste materials, testing various types of material in different conditions).

Fragmentation

Another possible difficulty is that sub-division of SOAs is conceived of only within individual curricular areas. Yet children do not operate within these tight curricular boxes. They may use mathematical knowledge in a science target. Ignoring the cross-fertilisation of ideas and skills from one curricular area to another could lead to an unnecessarily pedantic splitting of SOAs. This could also lead to a slowing down in the pace of the child's learning.

Focusing on programmes of study

These difficulties apply to attempts to sub-divide successive SOAs. Many of the problems do not apply if the teacher is focusing on level 1 only and asking: 'How can a child who is not yet at this level be helped to reach it?' The teacher can work back from level 1 as far as necessary and in as much or as little detail as is appropriate for a particular child. It is more positive to use level 1 as a broad initial level within which all children can, at minimum, be seen to be working, than to regard children who fall below level 1 attainments as 'off' the NC. Documentation about the NC has wavered between describing level 1 as meaning anything up to and including level 1 (i.e. level 1 as a broad phase) and level 1 as a specific 'benchmark' which children have not reached until they are able to complete a majority of the level 1 SOAs (this is discussed further in chapter 10).

At key stage 1, the planning of learning opportunities should take into account pre-infant school experiences. The report of the Rumbold Committee into the education and care of children under 5 has not been published at the time of writing. Provision for children with SEN was within the Committee's remit but it is likely that SEN will be addressed within broader equal opportunities issues. A crucial aspect will be the co-ordination of services for children under 5 who have been identified as having SEN. This co-ordination might involve Health, Education and care services in the public as well as the voluntary sectors. It is vital that there is not only co-ordination but also a direct link with the work of the reception class teacher.

PLANNING POSs FOR CHILDREN WITHIN LEVEL 1

A good starting point for the mainstream teacher of children with learning difficulties is to consider broadly a whole range of activities which might help a child to achieve early parts of the POSs.

English, AT 2: Reading

> The development of the ability to read, understand and respond to all types of writing, as well as the development of information-retrieval strategies for the purposes of study.
>
> (DES/WO 1990b: 7)

The associated POS is directed at the whole of key stage 1 and so includes a broad range of suggested activities. These include children listening to books, stories and poems; taking part in shared reading experiences with other children and the teacher, using texts composed and dictated by the children themselves; retelling, re-reading, or dramatising familiar stories and poems; making their own books, and talking about the way in which language is written down.

Teachers across LEAs and in cluster schools are working, often in groups, to plan how parts of POSs might be sub-divided. Some of their resultant lists have been published (e.g. Evans 1989) and various teacher magazines and journals (e.g. *Special Children*) report on similar materials. The list given below is the kind of thing that teacher groups are evolving.

POSs for children within level 1 on English AT 2 might include the following intermediate activities. These are not se- quential or comprehensive:

- Watching another child, or an adult, looking at a book,
- Sharing a book with an adult,
- Sharing a book with another child,

- Choosing a book to look at from a classroom book area,
- Hearing print in a familiar context, e.g. from a known story,
- Hearing print in an unfamiliar context, e.g. from a birth- day card,
- Activities linking the written symbols with meaningful messages, e.g. counting from a written list of names the numbers of children having school dinner,
- Collecting a variety of printed media (e.g. music scores, birthday cards, bottle labels) that convey information,
- 'Reading' a book in role play (later recognising rules concerning the direction of print),
- Letter/word games, e.g. finding the first letter of the child's name in other contexts (e.g. on road signs, in a teacher's name), at first with adult help then independ- ently,
- Decoding some basic sight vocabulary words from the daily environment (e.g. classroom, street, home),
- 'Playing' with rhyming words,
- Games involving recognising individual letter sounds in different contexts,
- Games involving identifying individual letter sounds in different contexts,
- Games involving recognising individual letter symbols in different contexts,
- Games involving identifying individual letter symbols in different contexts,
- Games involving matching individual letter sounds with their written symbols (and vice versa),
- Retelling to an adult, with some prompting, incidents from (and later the main story line) of a story, film or event,
- Retelling, without any adult prompting, a sequence of events,
- Inventing own stories stimulated by a variety of media (pictures, events, objects, dramatic play, etc.),
- Making own story and reading books using words/ sentences written by an adult but dictated by the child (building up from single word to simple sentences, and beyond).

In a lively classroom many of the usual activities associated with, for example, a listening corner, work in the local environment and (for younger children) play in a home corner or (for older children) drama-based activities, are likely to promote acquisition of these components. If a child seems to be having great difficulty in one or more of these activities, it would be appropriate to plan a structured teaching programme to promote learning in relation to the learning goals of that activity. For example, a child who does not enjoy books might be involved in a series of activities associated with listening skills. For example:

- Sharing music,
- Watching brief videos of simple stories,
- Handling books in various contexts (e.g. holding it for an adult to read),
- Looking at pictures/photographs with an adult.

Other examples of possible activities of early parts of POSs for children within level 1 are described below. In all cases these are tentative and intended only as starting points for discussion and planning teaching. The suggested activities do not form comprehensive or prescriptive lists, nor do they represent linear teaching sequences. They would provide markers to indicate how a child's learning is progressing. There are further examples in *A Curriculum for All* (NCC 1989d).

Science AT 1: Exploration of science

Children should be encouraged to develop their investigative skills and understanding of science in the context of explorations and investigations ... set within everyday experience of children.

(DES/WO 1989a: 65)

Possible activities in early parts of POSs include:

- Discussion about materials collected by the child,
- Discussion of adults' collections of objects based on a particular criterion (e.g. various foodstuffs all of which contain cinnamon),
- Games, with adult guidance, involving identifying certain sounds as higher/lower in pitch/tone than other sounds,
- Activities in which the child, prompted by an adult or friend, has to recognise certain tastes, scents, textures, pictures, having been told the identities of the items as a group (e.g. recognising, by their taste, sugar, lemon, curry),

- Games in which the child has to recall, without any hints, tastes, scents, textures, pictures (e.g. recalling, by their scent, An orange, a highly perfumed flower, wood).
- Paired discussion in which the child talks to a friend about an event,
- Group discussion in which the child tells a group of class-mates about an event,
- Independent 'projects' involving describing (to another child) what is happening (e.g. watching two colours mixing);
- Language games involving describing hidden objects to another child/group of children.

For a child who had difficulty in discussing groups of objects with an adult (the first two activities described above), additional activities such as the following might be developed:

- Making collections of some sort,
- Sharing a favourite object with an adult or another child.

Some of these activities could also be used as components of POSs towards other ATs; for example, Science, AT 14, level 1, relating to sound and music, and English AT 1, level 1, speaking and listening.

Mathematics AT 13: Handling data

Pupils should represent and interpret data.

(DES/WO 1989b: 35)

Possible activities in early parts of POSs for children within level 1 could include:

- Sorting objects with adult guidance; for example, sorting cutlery into the various sets of implements,
- Choosing sets containing more/less/the same number of objects,
- Completing simple mapping diagrams using picture cards (e.g. story book characters with appropriate object – fairy with wand, Father Christmas with sack of toys, a footballer with his team, a pop singer with his or her band), Initially with adult help then independently,
- Assembling a group of objects that belong together in some

way (e.g. making a shell collection) and explaining basis for
the grouping,
* Making a drawing of something seen around the school (e.g.
a bird at a bird table),
* Making drawings depicting things that go together (e.g. family
and clothes at a festival or special event),
* Playing games involving asking other children for more/ less,
same, ... and for things belonging with others.

For a child with persistent difficulties in sorting objects with adult
guidance (the first activity above), intermediate goals might
encompass these activities, carried out with an adult:

* Matching objects that are the same,
* Matching pictures that are the same,
* Matching by shape (2D and 3D),
* Matching by colour
* Matching by similarity of touch or sound (progressivly moving
from widely differing to less widely differing objects/pictures
on the key criterion),
* Matching objects that are different but have one key criterion
in common (e.g. different types of doll of which two have the
same colour dresses),
* Identifying the odd one out in a group (increasing the
number in the group and the magnitude of the differ- ence),

For all of these, there should be a move from recognition to recall,
e.g. 'Find me the one that matches this' to 'Can you find two that
match?'.

SUB-DIVIDING POSs WITHIN KEY STAGES 1 AND 2

The previous section has examined some ways of dividing early
parts of POSs into possible component activities for children within level 1. Not all children experiencing difficulties in learning in
primary schools will still be at that stage. Many will be between
(say) levels 1 and 2 of certain ATs. For example, a 9-year old may
be able to 'use pictures, [written] symbols or isolated letters, words
or phrases to communicate meaning' (English AT 3 writing, level
1; DES/WO 1990b: 12) but still be some way from producing
independently 'pieces of writing using complete sentences, some

of them demarcated with capital letters and full stops or question marks' (level 2).

The teacher has to find a way of helping a child move between these two levels, perhaps taking the whole of key stages 1 and 2 to do so. The same kind of process as that described earlier of identifying a series of activities, this time spanning several levels of an AT, will be needed. The starting point should be POSs or ATs rather than SOAs because of the problems of sequence and structure across SOAs, discussed earlier in this chapter. This applies across the foundation subjects, although the POSs for different subjects are written with different foci; for example, POSs in English and mathematics are written in terms of pupils' activities (i.e. what children might do), POSs for technology refer to what should be taught (i.e. curricular content), while science POSs describe teacher strategies. Interestingly, the POSs for technology list activities for each key stage and then list further activities according to level within the key stage, thereby giving a possible sub-division of targets into intermediate goals.

Sub-dividing parts of POSs is important because it will help the teacher to check that a child is making progress. Without such a sub-division a child may appear to be 'standing still' for long periods of time. Some examples of sub-divisions of POSs are given below.

English AT 4: Spelling

For key stage 1, the POS (DES/WO 1990b) includes the conventions of writing, the most common spelling patterns of consonant and short vowel sounds, the spelling of words which occur frequently in children's own writing, or which are important to them, and those which exemplify regular spelling patterns; and the names and order of letters of the alphabet.

How might a teacher begin to plan the curriculum for a child (say an 8-year old) who achieved level 1 in year 1 but has apparently had difficulty in learning the names and order of letters of the alphabet (i.e. progressing to level 2)? An initial step would be to try to list the amount that the child could do, relevant to this level 1 SOA. For example, the child might be identified as attaining level 1 but actually know only letter sounds and names of his name. This would involve making the kind of sub-division of the level 1 SOAs discussed in the previous section. Having done this, the teacher could clarify the extent to which the child could achieve the level

1 SOAs. Teaching could then carry on from the appropriate point. It would be useful to check acquisition and fluency of the aspects identified (as discussed in chapter 3). Perhaps progress to level 2 is slow because the child, although able to write letter sounds and names, is very cautious about this (for any of several reasons including hearing difficulties and lack of confidence).

Activities to develop English AT 4 (not a sequential or comprehensive list) could include:

- Writing letters with adult guidance, given the letter sound as the cue,
- Writing letters with adult guidance, given the letter name as the cue,
- Recognising individual letter sounds and names,
- Recalling individual letter sounds and names,
- Reading letter sounds, within words (as appropriate) with adult guidance,
- Matching individual letter shapes, with adult guidance,
- Writing letters with adult prompting, given the letter sound as the cue,
- Writing letters with adult prompting, given the letter name as the cue,
- Finding words in a simple picture dictionary, having been helped to locate the first letter,
- Writing words, given letter by letter sounding out by another child or by an adult,
- Writing words, given letter by letter names by another child or by an adult,
- Writing the first letter of words for classroom notices,
- Recognising whether words come in the first or last half of the dictionary/word book,
- Playing 'dictionary games' involving locating the correct page/section for a word,
- Independently finding words sought in simple picture dictionaries, then in unillustrated dictionaries,
- 'Sounding out' words for other children,
- Telling other children spellings using letter names,
- Using a variety of dictionaries and word books to find spellings,
- Using a variety of dictionaries and word books to find word meanings.

These activities would need to be part of a much wider, general English programme in the class so that the skills do not develop in isolation but within a context which gives them meaning.

At the start of this section, I referred to amount of adult help as being another way of thinking about planning intermediate goals. It will be evident that this dimension cross-references with the analysis of the activity, as outlined in the above examples. Although the two ways of breaking down tasks go side by side, it may be useful to bear the two distinct strategies in mind so that one or both are considered when children seem to find an activity difficult.

Planning intermediate goals is probably the most widely considered way of giving access to the NC to children who find learning difficult. It has the endorsement of the NCC's special needs working party (NCC 1989d) and has been taken up by practitioners. There are some basic points to bear in mind when planning intermediate goals:

- It is easier to apply this to some curricular areas than to others. Skills, in general, lend themselves to this approach whereas broader conceptual thinking does not.
- It is not possible to define categorically, in advance, 'correct' sequences of learning which will work for all children or even one specific child.
- Intermediate goals can be conceived in terms of amount and type of adult help as well as the nature of the activity.
- It is more effective to focus on POSs than SOAs, although in the Orders for some subjects (e.g. mathematics) the two are synonymous.

Dividing POSs into intermediate goals is one strategy to use in order to give children with learning difficulties access to the NC. This can help to show that those children are making progress, even if this is in small steps, towards the same ATs as other children. Some other ways of giving all children access to the NC are discussed in the next chapter.

Chapter 6

Helping children to gain access to the National Curriculum
Changing interest levels, presentation and response modes

'Cold callers' trying to sell products often fail because they have only one basic way of presenting their materials. The more sophisticated, and successful, sales people have a range of techniques which they use depending on the circumstances and reactions of the potential purchaser. Similarly, in teaching, effective teachers adjust their style to individual learners.

FOCUSING ON TOPICS WHICH MATCH THE CHILD'S INTEREST LEVELS

Fitting interest levels of children with the demands of particular activities is one way in which some children can be given greater access to the NC. One approach, often advocated in early childhood education, is to develop child-initiated work, often around a cross-curricular topic (Bruce 1987). This has been advocated on the grounds that subsequent work is more likely to interest the child if the starting point has been self-selected by the child, rather than imposed by the teacher. This approach dovetails with the discussion of using topic work to help generalisation and adaptation of knowledge and skills (discussed in chapter 3).

Parallel tasks: similar difficulty, different interests

In addition, specific parallel tasks can be planned so that, although the learning target is the same for a range of children, the means of promoting it reflect different interest levels. In a primary school, some 5-year olds, 7-year olds and 10-year olds might all be at a similar level on specific ATs but it would not be appropriate to use the same type of learning materials with all three groups. Some teachers (at class, school and/or LEA levels) are developing banks of such parallel activities which are linked with parts of the NC. The materials, while different in focus and perhaps style, are all aimed at developing the same AT. This is illustrated in the following examples of ATs or POSs with associated activities which are relevant to children with different interest levels.

Mathematics AT 13, Level 2 POS: Handling data

> Pupils should be constructing and interpreting frequency tables and block graphs.
>
> (DES/WO 1989b: 50)

Possible activities leading to this are, for a 7-year old:

- Graphing of months in which classmates have birthdays,
- Using large, coloured, sticky squares to build up block graphs representing, for example, eye colour of children in the class,
- Discussing similar charts compiled by other children or classes (e.g. shown in an assembly).

For a 9-year old:

- Making block graphs of types of vehicle passing the school (carried out in the course of a class project on transport), using 1 cm squared paper for recording,
- Interviewing school personnel (e.g. about area in which holidays were taken) and compiling a block graph from this information,
- Working in a team of children who have carried out this type of activity on related topics, (e.g. method of transport used to reach holiday destination, number of people in the holiday party) and discussing links across the block graphs (e.g. noticing any inconsistencies, such as if most people holiday in Cornwall and most people travel by air, there is probably something wrong with the graphs).

For an 11-year old:

- Collating information from classmates about their chosen secondary schools, using a micro-computer to build up the data base and print out the block graph,
- Listing numbers of goals scored by various footballers and

presenting this information in several ways, including block graphs,

- Using this as a basis for discussion with classmates about which players they would transfer/sell if they were the manager.

It is useful to think of a variety of contexts in which particular skills and knowledge could be developed, otherwise a child with difficulties in learning might experience, at different ages, very similar activities to promote particular ATs. Awareness of this problem has led to the development of teenage reading books with relatively low reading ages but with contents which are appropriate for a young person. Arguably, it is even more important to get the interest level right than it is to match the learning demands of the task with the child's capabilities. If the interest level is appropriate then the child may be sufficiently motivated to struggle through material which is too difficult.

This section has considered varying the context through which a task is developed by trying to match the interest level of the child with the focus of the task. The following sections discuss varying the ways in which, first, an activity is presented to a child and, second, a child might respond.

VARYING THE PRESENTATION OF ACTIVITY

A group of children may be working together on, say, making a weather station. The teacher could allow for children of different abilities within the group by varying the level of questions that he or she asks (see chapter 4, on multi-level tasks, for some specific examples) and by presenting the activities in different ways to children, depending on what is appropriate for individuals.

Teachers' questions/comments

Many teachers vary the level of talk, especially questions, directed to different children in ways which are intuitively tuned in to the varying ability levels of the children. This is one way of differentiating the task so that it is adjusted for different children. However, research on teachers' talk in classrooms (e.g. Wood *et al.* 1980, Tizard and Hughes 1984, Edwards and Westgate 1987, Wells 1987) suggests that teachers' talk is often not well attuned to individual children. In particular, it tends to be pitched too low in terms of linguistic and cognitive demands. This is no doubt related in part to the heavy managerial demands of the classroom. Teachers spend much of the time organising the class as a whole and have only brief exchanges with individual children. The NC may force attention on to the quality of teaching exchanges and encourage more careful matching of teachers' questions with children's cognitive levels. Many of the points raised in chapter 4 about adult's talk in child–adult conferences apply here also.

Presentation of activities

Another way of differentiating the task input so that it is matched to individual children is to use a range of media (tapes, microcomputers, workcards and task sheets, etc.). Thus, if children are, for example, relatively poor at reading, they may listen to instructions (from a tape or from another child) and so continue the activity. They are not prevented from following an activity just because, at the outset, they cannot gain access to it. This could be particularly important, if all classroom activities are mediated through English, for children for whom English is their second language.

Modifying written presentations of tasks

Many activities in primary classrooms start from written instructions on workcards, task sheets, a classroom notice or in workbooks. Much work has been carried out at secondary school level to modify worksheets, workcards and textbooks (referred to collectively here as 'written task sheets') for children with learning difficulties. Modifications have centred on reducing reading level without reducing content. There are relevant implications for planning written task sheets at key stages 1 and 2. Robin Lloyd-Jones (1985), Peter Croft (1989) and others have produced comprehensive advice about designing written task sheets for children who have difficulties in learning. The following checklist provides a guide to making or evaluating written task sheets:

- Use material that is within, or close to, the child's experience,
- Introduce new concepts in familiar contexts or settings,
- If possible, try out several versions of a written task sheet,
- Write in language that is easily understood,

- Leave a wide border all round the edge of the page,
- Highlight and explain new words,
- Use short sentences and simple sentence structure,
- Avoid ambiguous words,
- Provide plenty of clues, cues and examples,
- Give plenty of opportunities for success,
- Use type/print not handwriting,
- Use a print size compatible with the size of the children's handwriting,
- Use sub-headings to structure the written task sheet,
- Check that there are no more than ten words in each line for upper primary children and fewer than this for younger children,
- Use a simple, uncluttered layout,
- Use illustrations,
- Make sure that the illustrations tie in closely with the text,
- Differentiate clearly between text and instructions,
- Highlight instructions in some way (e.g. boxed),
- Use coloured as well as white paper (both for variety and for coding purposes, e.g. extension material on yellow paper) but be careful not to use certain combinations of ink and paper (e.g. red/orange with green/brown) as these may cause problems for children who are colour blind,
- Use active rather than passive verbs,
- Use pupils' contributions (e.g. a logo),
- Use pupils' feedback to decide whether or not the written task sheets fulfil your educational aims and objectives,
- Supplement with a taped version of the task sheet.

Problems of ambiguity in verbal instructions were discussed in chapter 4 in relation to child–adult conferences. Similar problems may be present in written material. The two workcards in Figures 6.1 and 6.2 (opposite) contain unintentional ambiguity, resulting in confusion and 'errors' for children who followed them literally.

VARYING CHILDREN'S MODES OF RESPONSE

Another strategy that may be used to help children with learning difficulties to participate in NC POSs is to examine different ways in which a child might develop and demonstrate abilities in particular POSs. Some SOAs specify that a particular activity must be oral

Figure 6.1 Workcard for water play during work on capacity
Children were given several jugs of different sizes, one jug of each size.

**How many little jugs fit into
the big jug?**

Figure 6.2 Workcard for a project on worms

Put the worm on a piece of paper.

Put a dot at each end of the worm.

Measure how long the worm is.

---

or, in other cases, written. However, there is considerable scope for using children's strongest aspects of learning to promote attainments.

Varying modes of response: integrating this into teaching plans

Children with difficulties in learning may have problems with reading and writing but may be very competent in practical tasks. Science and technology POSs may, in particular, lend themselves to being developed orally and practically for children with learning difficulties, although classmates may use written methods. Some history and geography targets could be developed through role play. Science, technology and mathematics could be fostered through the child manipulating concrete materials and showing/describing the result to an adult rather than writing down the findings. This stance is supported by HMI's survey of children with SEN in mainstream schools, which noted: 'Work of at least satisfactory quality was often associated with experience-based learning activities which used a range of media and practical activities' (HMI 1989b: para. 15).

This point is illustrated by examining some extracts from POSs. In science, at key stage 2, children should be encouraged to formulate testable hypotheses (DES/WO 1989c). Children with poor reading levels may have difficulty in demonstrating this if the work requires reading instructions from a book or workcard. This does not mean that the child is unable to make the scientific judgements but that he or she is prevented from showing this because the means of communication is based on a weakness, for the child, not a strength. If, instead, work towards this part of the POS involved the child in a large amount of firsthand experience, including discussion of results with classmates, then such scientific understanding might well be demonstrated.

Children who find school-based learning difficult may need to manipulate concrete materials in order to understand the basic concepts. Although this is a regular part of early learning it may be more difficult to find ways of introducing concrete materials into activities with older children, particularly if the materials are perceived as 'babyish'. Anne Henderson (1989) has described the sets of concrete materials which she made to help children to grasp concepts about place value. She made blocks to represent not just hundreds, tens and units (as in Dienes apparatus) but also three-dimensional 'decimal points' and blocks to represent one-tenth and one-hundredth. She gives an interesting account of games which she devised using these concrete materials. She believes that they were highly effective in developing both mathematical understanding and self-confidence about maths. Similar approaches can be developed in other aspects of the curriculum.

Varying children's mode of response in topic work

Many primary schools use topic- or project-based approaches, within or across curricular areas, and these can be planned so that there are parallel activities in which children with learning difficulties participate alongside classmates. The trend seems to be towards topics which are closely, although not exclusively, subject based. Gone are the days of the vast topic web in which anything and everything which could conceivably be linked to some key theme was included in the project. One impact of the NC is the demise of the multi-subject topic. This was signalled in Eric

Bolton's statement in his annual report: 'The weakest work in primary school occurs when too many aspects of different subjects are roped together within integrated themes or topic work' (HMI 1990b: para. 36). The move away from multi-subject topics is reflected also in the use of HMI's areas of learning and experience as the basis for curriculum planning (discussed in chapter 3)

Some possible parallel activities are outlined below for two typical primary school projects: 'Growth' and 'Shops'. (A similar approach is described more fully, in relation to a topic on 'Shipwreck', in Lewis and Thorpe 1989.) These parallel activities reflect flexibility and diversity in both possible presentation of activities and/or children's type of response.

Topic: Growth

This is a science-based topic but involves also mathematics, English, technology and art.

Possible activities include:

- Children could plant various things and monitor how they grow. Children with difficulties in learning could be encouraged to record observations by telling another child and/or by speaking into a tape recorder or *Language Master* machine, rather than necessarily making written recordings of observations. These could be developed as part of role playing the various parts of scientist, reporter, scribe, etc.
- Observational drawings could be made by all children. Children with difficulties could begin by making representational paintings rather than more precise drawings.
- All children could make paintings of impressions of, for example, woods, meadowland or grass, aiming to capture the 'feel' of the environment rather than actuality. (Music such as Vivaldi's *Four Seasons* could be used as a stimulus).
- All children could look for relevant non-fiction books. If necessary, children with reading difficulties could share these with a competent child or adult in order to discover information.
- All children, but particularly those with learning difficulties, could use micro-computer based simulation programs to develop ideas about plant requirements.
- Computer data bases could be built up by the children collectively and used in various ways depending on children's mathematical skills and knowledge.

- Children could work in pairs of similar ability to devise apparatus to monitor aspects of plant growth. One pair of children might appropriately monitor rate of growth, devising a simple stand with horizontal scale; another pair might plan to monitor plant respiration. In this way children of widely varying attainments could be included in parallel activities and make complementary contributions to overall conclusions.
- Children could invent and model, or draw, their own versions of 'useful' plants, such as, a plant to collect wasps or, much more complex, a plant which could survive in an atmosphere with limited oxygen.
- A group or class book on growing things could contain contributions from a range of children. Children with learning difficulties could do illustrations: they could find, cut out from magazines and paste in relevant photographs or make print pictures using various seeds, bulbs or leaves. They could write short contributions including, for example, a contents page and parts of a glossary. Word procesors and desk top printing packages could be used as well as, or instead of, handwritten material.
- Children could make collections of folk and fairy tales which are related to growing things. Some children could find these by reading a range of fiction. Children without sufficient reading abilities could interview adults and children (inside and outside the class) to make an oral collection of such stories.
- Whole class discussion about differences in rates of growth could include reflections about visual and sensory impairments. This could help children to recognise the continuum of normality.

Topic: Shops

This is a geography/history-based topic but involves also English, mathematics, art and technology.

Possible activities include:

- Children could use photographs, taken over a period of time, as the foci of discussion about changes in the area. Similarly, artefacts could stimulate discussion, conjecture and problem solving among children with a range of attainments. Some children could compose 'headlines' for the photographs while other children write accompanying stories, depending on levels of interest, skill and motivation.

- Children could write accounts of what the shops used to be like. (If they are a recent development, the accounts might be about the area prior to the shops being built.) Children with difficulties in writing could dictate their accounts to an adult for writing, record their accounts on a tape recorder, or record changes pictorially through drawings or collections of news photographs.
- Children could role play various occupations associated with the running of a shop. Children could be divided into groups so that complexity of role is appropriate for the child. Relatively simple roles might include sales person, purchaser, delivery driver or cash till operator. More complex roles could include accountant, buyer, store detective, tax inspector, general manager, personnel officer, so that the topic is demanding of able children in the group or class as well as being appropriate for less able children.
- Role play and drama could include various purchasing simulations. Whether or not coins are available and the type of coins used will depend on the children's levels. Some children might use, say 5p, 10p and 20p coins while other children, in separate but parallel activities, might use the whole range of coins and notes. Yet other children might carry out transactions using 'cheques' (e.g. with the sales person mentally totalling the cost of goods and the purchaser writing out the 'cheque').
- A favourite shop could be selected and the source traced of chosen items. This would involve use of reference material and/or interviews with shopkeepers. Children with learning difficulties might do more of the oral work and fewer written activities than other children.
- Observational drawings could be made of the shops (interiors and/or exteriors) and associated people, with children using media (e.g. paint, wax crayon, pastel crayon, chalk, charcoal, drawing pencil) appropriate to their abilities and experiences.
- Working models could be designed of, for example, trolleys to transport goods from delivery areas to shelves, conveyor belts to move goods across the checkout, and children's own inventions such as a machine to shop in a supermarket on behalf of an elderly person. Children with difficulties could be

encouraged to develop relatively simple models (e.g. a shop-
ping trolley or cart) while children with a good understanding
of mechanical things could try to develop more complex
models, such as a robot shopper.

- Children could interview various adults working in the shops,
in order to develop both ideas about the various roles and
knowledge of the background to products. If children were to
prepare the interview questions beforehand then all children
could be involved in asking the questions. In mixed ability
groups more able children could construct appropriate record
sheets and summary forms.

- Children could invent orally, read and/or write a range of
stories associated with shops. These might be relatively factual
(e.g. accounts of a day in the life of a shop worker) or based
on fantasy (e.g. a shop with a magic doormat). These kinds of
activity could be carried out by all children at their own levels.

- Maps could be made to show the location of the shops. The
sophistication of these would vary with children's abilities and
understanding. Children with difficulties could be encouraged to begin by laying acetate sheets over aerial photographs
and drawing over the route, thus helping them to develop an
understanding that maps represent real features.

- Accounts of changes in the shops could be written by children
with learning difficulties by using successive cartoon-style
boxes, with limited writing.

- Children could invent board games showing change in the
area (e.g. one square represents 10 years). Children of all
abilities could contribute to this type of activity.

- Coins from different countries could be collected and
analysed, divided into different sets on the basis of one, two or
three criteria (e.g. size, shape, age, continent). This could lead
to observational drawing. Both types of activity could be done
at various levels of ability.

- The whole class could discuss adaptions in shops which would
aid people with disabilities.

Many of these suggestions involve, as found in numerous primary
schools, a strong emphasis on firsthand experience and oral
means of communciation. Varying the mode of chidren's responses, as described in these examples, may apply also to assessments
of learning.

Varying the mode of response when assessing learning

Assessments of learning may be carried out through various channels, not just the immediately obvious, written tasks. For example, in Technology AT 1, level 2, children should be able to 'describe what they have observed or visualised and found out in their exploration' (DES/WO 1990c: 3). This could be done by verbal, pictorial, modelled and/or written accounts, without moving away from the AT. A number of the ATs can be assessed through means other than written presentation. An over-reliance on children's written responses can easily lead to an under-estimation of children's knowledge and skills. In turn, this under-estimation is likely to lead to teaching which is aimed at too low a level for the child.

However, some ATs specify the type of response required. For example, English AT 3, writing, level 2 requires children to 'Write stories showing an understanding of the rudiments of story structure' (DES/WO 1990b: 12). This might be developed in various ways, including oral story telling or inventing cartoon-style story sequences. However, assessment of this AT would need to be in written not oral form (unless the AT were formally modified for the child). The final part of this chapter brings together the strategies described here and the planning of intermediate goals, discussed in chapter 5, by describing two case studies showing ways in which the teacher might help children with difficulites in learning to gain access to specific aspects of the NC.

An example: Melvin

Melvin is 9 years old but his reading is at the level of an average 6/7-year old. Other school attainments are, like his reading, 'behind' that of his peers. He has no special hobbies or interests but is enthusiastic about the *Ghostbusters* stories on television.

Action:

Melvin's class teacher has been using the *Ginn 360* reading scheme with Melvin but he has made little progress. The class teacher feels that this may be because he associates these books with his unsuccessful attempts to read. She has tried the *Breakthrough* materials but he is not enthusiatic about these because he says that they are 'babyish'.

The teacher decides to concentrate on one curricular area with Melvin. His main difficulties are in reading and this hampers other learning so, although his writing is also poor, she decides to focus on reading. She identifies Melvin as being past level 1 and near to level 2 in reading. The class teacher assesses Melvin in relation to each of the level 2 SOAs; he can read many of the signs and notices in the classroom, has some understanding of alphabetical order, uses picture but not context cues in his reading and has a very poor recall of events in a story although he seems to enjoy hearing stories. The range of reading material which he can and will read unprompted is very limited. After this assessment the teacher decides to concentrate on developing Melvin's enjoyment, and recall, of stories.

Breaking down the task

The teacher identifies a series of activities which she hopes will develop Melvin's enjoyment and recall of stories. These activities, recorded on teaching plans and later on record sheets, are:

- Watching a video of a short story (the topic chosen by Melvin),
- Drawing a picture of one event from the story,
- Re-telling to a friend or adult what is happening in the picture,
- Responding to questions about what led up to and/or followed from the event depicted,
- Placing in sequence a series of pictures about the taped story (if the story is seen or heard by some of the other children in the class then the pictures could be supplied by them or, if the story tape is commercially available, published sets of pictures might be available),
- Re-enacting with friend(s) the events in the story,
- Drawing a series of cartoon-style pictures to record key events in the story in sequence, starting with a series of three boxes and gradually increasing the number of boxes,
- Writing, with a friend and perhaps using a word processor, an account of the story but with one or two key events changed,
- Partnering a younger or less able child to whom he tells this story.

The teacher plans to use several different stories if Melvin becomes bored with the first story.

Matching interest level

If Melvin chooses the story, perhaps bringing in a video from home of a favourite story or series, then the activity is likely to be motivating for him because the interest level of the story/stories will be appropriate.

Alternative ways of presenting the task

The activities outlined above involve a variety of ways of presenting the task. None of them involves reading at this stage although this could be added when Melvin has completed the activities successfully.

Alternative modes of responding

The activities outlined above involve a variety of responses from Melvin but relatively little writing, which is one of his weak areas. Writing will be the focus of a separate teaching plan.

An example: Amanda

Amanda is an 8-year old who is, in general, at level 2 on most of the SOAs in the core subjects. Her general knowledge is quite good compared with peers but she has difficulty in various activities which involve spatial awareness and understanding. For example, she is often confused about her right- and her left-hand sides, she makes mistakes when trying to follow directions involving right and left, she confuses compass directions and finds drawing simple maps difficult. Amanda's care-givers have reported that she has had these types of difficulties for some time. Her favourite activity at home is playing with a puppet theatre made by an uncle.

The teacher is planning a topic related to the local environment. This will include drawing maps of the local area (Geography AT 1) and the teacher anticipates that Amanda will find it difficult to complete some of the activities. None of the children has worked extensively on this topic before as it is not in the school's scheme of work until year 3.

Action

Amanda's class teacher organises a discussion and preliminary activities with the whole class to assess how much they know in relation to this AT. She finds that Amanda can carry out some of the level 1 activities (draw round simple objects to show shape in plan) and one level 2 task (identify land and sea on maps and globes). She cannot complete any of the related SOAs at levels 1 or 2.

Breaking down the task

The teacher plans the following activities:

- Recognising objects from their silhouettes (e.g. using shadows thrown up by an OHP),
- Recognising objects on an outline plan,
- Drawing several non-overlapping objects in outline,
- Recognising overlapping objects on an outline plan,
- Making a 3D model of something in a picture or photograph,
- Drawing front/rear views of a 3D object,
- Tracing a picture (i.e. a 'front' view),
- Drawing an aerial view of a 3D object.

Matching interest level

As Amanda is very interested in and enthusiastic about puppets, her teacher could use this interest to develop Amanda's mapping skills. Amanda could make a small puppet theatre from junk materials as part of craft activities and then the various aspects of plan making, which are identified above, could be carried out using the puppet theatre as the focus. This could involve, for example, drawing the puppet theatre as it appears to her looking down from above, as it appears to friends watching from the front and as it appears to someone watching from behind the puppet theatre. The puppet theatre activities could include shadow as well as 3D puppets and so help to develop Amanda's linking of 2D and 3D objects. She could go on to write plays for the puppets and these could involve directions about where the puppets have to move to and from. A range of 'director's materials' could show the plan of the stage, movements, etc.

Alternative ways of presenting the task/alternative modes of responding

The various puppet play activities involve a wide range of ways of presenting of the task and types of response from Amanda. Written plans are drawn only at a relatively late stage.

Chapters 2 to 6 have looked at planning teaching and how, specifically, this planning can help children with difficulties in learning to have access to the NC and a broader curriculum beyond that. The next chapter moves the focus to the grouping of children in the classroom.

Chapter 7

Grouping of children

The basis on which children could be divided into teaching groups is an aspect of the NC which has aroused controversy in relation to children with difficulties in learning. The first part of this chapter will review and evaluate what is being suggested regarding this topic in NC statutory and advisory documents. The second part focuses on implications for practice, including a particular aspect of the grouping of children: the integration of children from special schools and units into mainstream settings.

The NC lays down a framework of what should be taught at various stages and how this should be assessed but does not state the way in which it should be taught. In this respect the English and Welsh national curricula are less rigid than the national curricula that are developed in some other countries. These, by stipulating some aspects of teaching method, such as the pacing of work and teaching materials, are more prescriptive. However, there are, in some POSs and ATs, indications about teaching method. In particular, the group work that is required in some POSs and ATs would be difficult to carry out in a highly traditional classroom which was dominated by rows of desks facing the front of the classroom.

Teaching method encompasses the approach to curriculum planning (e.g. single-subject based, cross-curricular or a mixture of these), teaching materials (e.g. reading schemes, 'real' books, concrete mathematics equipment, materials for science experiments) and how the class is organised (e.g. integrated day, mixed or single ability groups). To date, commentaries and advice about teaching method and the NC have focused mainly on the first two of these three aspects. Several LEAs and primary school interest groups are producing guidelines on planning topic work in the NC and publishers are advertising schemes which aim to teach successive levels of individual NC subjects. Relatively little discussion has taken place about classroom organisation, and specifically the grouping of children, in relation to teaching the NC.

RECOMMENDATIONS IN NC DOCUMENTS CONCERNING GROUPING OF CHILDREN FOR TEACHING

There are two issues about the grouping of children for teaching which arise from NC documentation. One issue concerns the delimiting of levels and corresponding key stages. In the Orders for English, Mathematics, Science, and Technology and the proposals for History and Geography, key stage 2 (8–11 year olds) starts at level 2. Eight to 11-year olds who are at level 1 are below the boundary of what has been designated, on the basis of chronological age, to be the appropriate key stage. Setting these statutory limits creates problems about what to do about the children who fall outside those boundaries.

The second issue concerns how children are grouped for teaching. This falls outside the NC, as it is a matter of teaching method not curriculum content. Teaching method, as Kenneth Baker and then John McGregor often reiterated, is a matter for individual schools, rather than central government, to decide. Nevertheless the DES has commented on pupil grouping and supports a mix of age and ability grouping. This contrasts with advice from the NCC, which has been more cautious about advocating ability grouping. Discussion of grouping by the level that is reached on SOAs leads to questions about children repeating a year (a system termed *redoublement* in France).

Implications of a mismatch between key stage and NC level

The organisation of individual subjects in the NC is based on three strands which are assumed to coincide. The three strands are key stage, chronological age and NC level. For example:

Key stage 1: 5–7 year olds Levels 1–3
Key stage 2: 8–11 year olds Levels 2–5
                          or 2–6 (mathematics only)

Most children will be working on a level within their appropriate key stage. This will be the case for children with difficulties in learning at key stage 1 if level 1 is interpreted very broadly to mean anything up to and including level 1. Children at key stage 2 who are on level 1 are, in theory, outside the levels specified by the Orders for their age group. The setting of limits means that some way has to be found to legitimate the work of children who fall below (or above) the limits. This is relatively straightforward for children who have statements, since the children can, through the statement, be exempted from specified ranges of work. For children who have difficulties in learning but do not have statements:

> It will be possible for pupils to be taught for part of the time (perhaps as much as half or more) at levels *below those specified for their key stage, so long as they work on programmes of study material specified for their key stage during the latter part of the key stage.*
>
> (NCC 1989d: 10; my emphasis)

This is an interpretation of two paragraphs (36 and 37) from Circular 6/89 (DES 1989b). It changes the emphasis slightly from the original Circular. First, there is a difference in the amount of non-key stage appropriate work which is implied as being permissible. The NCC talks of this as being 'perhaps as much as half *or more*'. However, the Circular states that children should be '*mainly* taught POS material within the levels appropriate for his or her key stage' and therefore implies that non-key stage appropriate work cannot be more than half.

Another difference concerns the shift, mentioned by the NCC, in the proportion of key-stage related work across the key stage. NCC states that appropriate key stage work must be taught at the end of the key stage. Circular 6/89 does not differentiate between how appropriate key stage work is spread across the key stage. What the NCC seems to have done is to interpret the Circular as referring to key stage appropriate work as a whole but, within this, the letter of the Circular could be adhered to by doing more key stage appropriate work at the end, and less at the beginning of the key stage. To work out what this means in practice, if this interpretation is correct, imagine the position for Melanie who has learning difficulties (working, crudely, at about three years below the level of her mainstream peers). The possible balance of key stages 1 and 2 work for Melanie during the four years of junior schooling (i.e. 'key stage 2') might be:

Year 3: 70% key stage 1 material and 30% key stage 2 material
Year 4: 50% key stage 1 material and 50% key stage 2 material
Year 5: 40% key stage 1 material and 60% key stage 2 material
Year 6: 35% key stage 1 material and 65% key stage 2 material

This type of arrangement would meet the Circular's demands for appropriate key stage work for most of the key stage but, because of the way in which this has been distributed, Melanie can still have a relatively high proportion of key stage 1 work in years 3 and 4. This example is of course theoretical and it would be complex, although feasible, to translate into practice. This arrangement would make it possible and reasonable for Melanie to stay with her age mates in a mixed ability class as she moves through key stage 2.

Grouping of children into teaching groups

Class grouping by NC level

Some of the issues about grouping children by attainments on NC levels and 'norms' for each age group stem from the TGAT Report's (DES/WO 1988a) graph (see figure 7.1) showing the hypothesised sequence of ten levels of attainment in the NC for age groups of children between 7 and 16.

The dotted vertical lines show the hypothesised spread of attainments of 80 per cent of children at the specified ages. The TGAT Report's recognition of the spread of levels at any one age has been played down in subsequent NC documentation. This is illustrated by the definition of level 2 as the lower boundary of key stage 2. The TGAT diagram covers only 80 per cent of each age group, so 20 per cent will, hypothetically, be above or below the areas shown. Consequently, the actual spread of attainments would be even wider than those shown in figure 7.1.

The NC structure of hierarchies of SOAs at ten levels might be interpreted as encouraging the use of NC levels as the bases for teaching groups. Associated continuous teacher assessments will identify children as being, broadly, at one of ten levels in any particular subject. As each level in the NC was envisaged by the TGAT Report (DES/WO 1988a) as representing two years of age, classes based on levels could still contain a wide range of attainment. Consequently, considerable differentiation of work within the class would still be necessary (see chapters 5 and 6). However,

Figure 7.1 Sequence of pupil achievement of levels between ages
7 and 16
The bold line gives the expected results for pupils at the ages specified.
The dotted lines represent a rough speculation about the limits within
which about 80 per cent of the pupils may be found to lie.

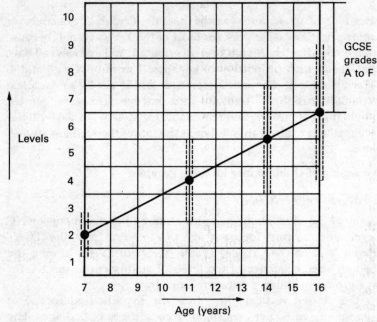

Source: TGAT Report (DES/WO 1988a: para. 104)

the range of attainments would be likely to be less wide than that
found previously in most primary classes. The Cockcroft Report
(DES 1982) referred to a typical spread of attainments of seven
years in classes of 11-year olds (year 6).

There are many difficulties associated with treating levels on
SOAs as the basis for allocating children to classes. (Their use in
relation to 'setting' children within or across classes is considered
below.) The first set of difficulties concerns determining an NC-
based attainment level for a child. All of the child's attainments
would have to be reduced to some single figure in order to decide
which class a child should join. For example, if classes were based
on single NC levels, how would a place in a (say) level 3 class be
determined? Would this relate to only the core subjects and what
if attainment levels in the core subjects varied? It might be argued
that a child in a level 3 class would have a majority of attainments

at level 3 but some attainments might be seen as more central than others. Would allocation to classes be determined by, say, level on English targets because these might be said to underlie all other attainments? If this were the case it would disadvantage children for whom English is a second language. Would children be moved around mid-year to make adjustments for those who had, for example, already progressed to level 4?

Even if these kinds of argument could be resolved satisfactorily, one is attributing a spurious accuracy to NC levels by using them as the basis for placement. The differences between levels assigned to similar activities in different subjects (e.g. science and geography), apparent large gaps between successive levels, and doubtful sequences of levels in some ATs (e.g. mathematics) mean that levels are not highly precise and 'accurate'. The specification of levels in the ATs remain best guesses until the NC has been tried out.

The second set of difficulties concerning streaming children on the basis of NC levels relates to children's wider development. If there is a 'level 2' class in a primary school then, in theory, this might contain a majority of 7-year olds plus some younger children with relatively high attainments for their ages and some older children with relatively low attainments for their ages. The chronological spread might easily range from 5-year olds to 9-year olds. A child with learning difficulties might remain at one level for a relatively long time (perhaps four or five years compared with two years for peers). A child with severe learning difficulties who is integrated into a mainstream primary school operating this system could, theoretically, end up spending almost all of his or her school career in a level 1 class while successive groups of normal peers ripple past him or her. There could be enormous developmental differences between, for example, able 5-year olds, 'average' 7-year olds and 9-year olds with learning difficulties, in spite of similarities in attainment terms. To group these children together for teaching makes sense only if academic development is the sole consideration. If personal and social development are also to be fostered then class grouping on the basis of similarities in curricular attainments becomes of questionable value.

Despite these difficulties, the DES seems to be moving towards streaming and away from a flexible system of varying groupings for different subject areas. Circular 5/89 (issued in February 1989) refers to the possibility that:

An individual pupil might, however, be younger or older [than the majority of pupils in a class or teaching group].... This enables a pupil to be taught with another age group for *one or more* subject areas where appropriate.

> (DES 1989a: para. 33; my emphasis)

More strongly, *From Policy to Practice,* issued May 1989, states:

Individual pupils can, as some do now, work with a class of older or younger pupils, for some or *all* subjects.

> (DES 1989d: para. 8.2; my emphasis)

The NCC is more cautious, stating that children with or without statements may be in a teaching group of younger pupils but that: 'It is the view of NCC that this option will not often be practicable or educationally desirable and will be kept under review' (NCC 1989d: 10). Martin Davies, director of the NCC, has reinforced this stance: 'There is no need for remedial classes and there is no need for pupils to be taught in groups of a different age ... we don't want the dynamic to move in the direction of level 1 remedial groups' (NCC 1989e: 3). On similar lines, HMI, in their review of children with statements in ordinary schools (HMI 1990c) are more positive about grouping these children with other mainstream pupils on the basis of chronological age rather than by attainment.

Streaming, at primary or secondary school levels, is likely to be detrimental for children with learning difficulties. A consistent finding in research into streaming is that it diminishes the self-esteem of children in 'lower' streams. In an extensive review of the effects of streaming on cognitive aspects of development (Cronbach and Snow 1977), it is emphasised that dividing children into streams and teaching them separately can only be justified if this separation can be shown to be more effective than when the children are taught together. They conclude that the research evidence is equivocal and does not support streaming as a means of improving academic learning for the whole ability range.

The possibility of redoublement

In theory, the concept of *redoublement* cannot be applied to the operation of the NC because it contains no notion of absolute pass and fail. Children are judged against several series of curriculum-based assessments. However, the levels are being interpreted by some LEAs as precise and normative. This has opened the way for the argument that some children will 'fail' to meet a norm (e.g. level 4 at age 11) and so will need to re-take earlier work. Wandsworth has advocated streaming on the basis of children's levels on SOAs and has extended this, saying that children will have to re-take a year if they do not reach satisfactory levels. The firmest proposals which have been reported have focused on secondary school level and state that, in Wandsworth, children in comprehensive schools (as part of a wider magnet schools policy) will be 'judged and streamed according to academic progress and not by age ... pupils [will have] to repeat lessons if their target attainment is not met' (Bates 1990a). Education officials reportedly recognise that such an approach could lead to some secondary school classes containing children with a three or four year spread in ages.

Wandsworth, by planning for streaming and the repeating of a year if a child has 'failed', is taking a more extreme line than that given explicitly in DES statements. The DES has not advocated making children who 'fail' a year repeat the year. However, the point is phrased negatively and weakly: 'There is nothing in the ERA to require pupils to repeat a year, nor to prevent an early move to another year group' (Circular 15/89, DES 1989e: para. 33). The tone of Circular 15/89 was strengthened in a later Circular (3/90) in which a similar statement to that given above was followed by: '*except where the school judges this to be in the best interests of the pupil*' (DES 1990c: para. 23 ii; my emphasis). Such a justification could be applied very widely and could be defended, by a determined LEA or school, on so many different grounds that opponents would have a hard time defeating such justifications. The emphasis should be on finding appropriate teaching approaches rather than assuming that children who 'fail' to meet certain criteria need merely to repeat methods which have been demonstrably unsuccessful.

Setting and within-class grouping of children

The document, *A Framework for the Primary Curriculum* (NCC 1989c), considers the issue of grouping of pupils and reviews the varieties and purposes of different forms of grouping. It does not favour any specific form of grouping and concludes: 'The clarity of the National Curriculum subject requirements and detailed information about pupils' achievements will allow teachers to ensure grouping arrangements are made appropriately. At all times, the needs of the individual pupil should be given the highest priority' (NCC 1989c: 11). The emphasis is on using different forms of grouping as appropriate and that 'there may be occasions' on which it is appropriate for able children to work with older children. This stance accords well with evidence from various research (e.g. the ORACLE project, Galton *et al.* 1980) which also advocated flexibility in classroom groupings and a mix of individual, small group and whole class work. The NCC's advisory document on the NC and special needs (NCC 1989d) also states that good learning environments will be characterised by flexible groupings.

Mixed ability classes with some setting into work groups of children at similar levels of attainment within the class or across several classes would avoid many of the difficulties associated with allocating children to fixed class groups according to NC level. However, the need to be tentative about levels still applies if these are used as the basis for planning work groups within the class. It is easier to retain this tentativeness if groupings are flexible. Apparent anomalies (e.g. 'This child comes out at level 3 in maths but there are still some level 2 activities which he needs to develop') can be allowed for ('On Mondays he joins red group for level 2 work on money, on the other days he does maths with blue group who are working on level 3 number').

Some ATs explicitly require that the target is developed through children working with other children. For example, in English (AT 1, level 2), pupils should be able to 'participate as speakers and listeners in a group engaged in a given task'. Similarly, Technology (AT 3, level 4) states that pupils should be able to work with others in the planning and apportioning of tasks. More commonly, ATs do not require group working but this is suggested as a way of developing the target. There are many examples of this in the English, Science, Technology, Geography and History documents. The History proposals (DES 1990d), for example, advocate drama, role play, re-enactments and simulations as ways of bringing history to life and developing senses of time and place. Teachers might of course choose to teach programmes of study using group learning experiences even when these are not explicitly required or suggested. In Mathematics, for example, children might work as a group in developing and explaining bar charts, although that target or corresponding programme of study does not refer to group work.

IMPLICATIONS FOR PRACTICE

Sarah Tann (1988) makes a useful distinction between the grouping of children that is an organisational matter, such as seating children around tables, and those work groups in which children work collaboratively. The two aspects of grouping are not synonymous. Children in primary classrooms are often seated in groups but work independently (Galton *et al.* 1980, Tizard *et al.* 1988). It is the second aspect, working groups, which is considered here.

Working groups based on children with similar levels of attainment in particular aspects of the NC

Some areas of the curriculum are likely, for at least some of the time, to be developed by children working in groups with others at similar attainment levels. The individuals in these groups are likely to vary across different subjects and even within a subject. Although it might be easier in organisational terms to have children in the same broad ability-based groups for all curricular areas, most primary teachers do vary the children in different groups. This helps to avoid the labelling of children and encourages all children to see themselves, and to be seen, as able to do well at some things.

It might be argued that one disadvantage of the shared NC for all children is that it makes it more obvious that, especially in a mixed ability class, some children (or perhaps only one child) may be carrying out the kind of work which classmates had completed a year or more previously. However, before the NC had begun, children as young as 5 or 6 rapidly realised the relative academic standing of classmates. This occurred even in mixed ability classes in which teachers had tried not to draw attention to children's different levels of attainment. In one study (Crocker and Cheeseman 1988), 141 infant school children were asked to rate every child in their classes as better or worse than themselves. There was a strong agreement between self, classmates' and teacher's rankings and from the age of 6 onwards, spontaneous rankings tended to be based on academic criteria. This supports what teachers often suspect: the academically less able children in the class tend to be quickly labelled as such by themselves, classmates and the teacher. This puts a responsibility on the teacher not to reinforce such rankings and to recognise the need to be consistently positive towards a child. Frequent, small, correct steps can be praised while large, incorrect steps can easily lead to a cycle of negative feedback, despair and further negative feedback.

It was common practice in the 1960s and 1970s to withdraw from the classroom children with particular difficulties. Withdrawal group work focused on intensive teaching, usually related to reading, and was often carried out by a peripatetic reading teacher who was not on the school staff. This practice came into disfavour because gains made in withdrawal groups were not sustained once children returned full time into ordinary classes. Other disadvantages of the withdrawal group system for children with learning difficulties are that those children miss out on normal classroom activities while they are withdrawn elsewhere, and they may experience conflicting teaching approaches and a lack of continuity in curricular content. The withdrawal group system also took attention away from the normal classroom in which the children still spent most of their time, so that ways of helping the child within the classroom (for example, by ensuring that classroom notices could be interpreted by all children) were not tackled. In addition, responsibility for children with learning difficulties came to be seen as outside the work of class teachers and, arising from this, was excluded from issues about whole school policy.

These difficulties have led to a move away from withdrawal group work and towards an emphasis on helping all class teachers to meet the needs of children with difficulties in learning. Special needs 'support' teachers now often work in the classroom alongside the class teacher. However, research by Caroline Gipps and others (1987) found that primary teachers favoured withdrawal group work. It was the second most preferred strategy as a way to help children with SEN; only smaller classes were seen as a more useful strategy. The placing of these two strategies first and second is probably a reflection of the huge demands on teachers' time in normal classroom life. Anything which relieves these demands, such as having fewer children around, is likely to be welcomed. It seems that the in-class support movement is working against strong enthusiasm for withdrawal group work but discussion among school staff may clarify for whose benefit the withdrawal group work is taking place!

For some children there may be a case for their working in a small group with a special needs teacher, perhaps outside the classroom, for part of the time. A study of children with communication problems in reception classes (Clark *et al.* 1984) lends support for some intensive small group work on language outside the classroom. The common framework provided by the NC should help this type of activity by giving a structure of continuity and progression. The central issues are not about where the children work but about the degree of continuity across different teachers and a belief that all teachers have responsibility for children with SEN. It is vital that, if children do participate in group work outside the classroom, one person (for example, the class teacher) retains a clear role as co-ordinator and manager of all the work in which each child is engaged. This is considered further in chapter 8.

Working groups based on children with a range of attainments

Some activities lend themselves to being developed in groups in which children fulfil different roles and the breadth of attainments and interests is an asset both in cognitive and social terms. If children in a lower attainment group for one subject are in mixed attainment groups for other curricular areas then the problems of lowered self-esteem found in streaming are less likely to occur. Some primary schools are deliberately increasing mixed aged, and by implication mixed ability, classes in order to spread the load of assessments to be made at the reporting ages. For example, where years 1 and 2 children or years 5 and 6 children are grouped together, the teacher is involved in making SATs assessments on only some of the children in the class. If all year 2 or year 6 children are in single age group classes then their teachers have to make SATs assessments on the whole class during a relatively brief period (see chapter 10).

Mixed attainment groups are important for children's personal and social development and should be used for at least some classroom activities. As children do work out the differences in the relative academic standing of classmates, it seems futile to try to pretend that these do not exist. A more positive response is to foster a classroom climate in which there is an acceptance that all children (and adults) have strengths and weaknesses and individual differences are recognised, not ignored.

A further advantage of mixed attainment work groups occurs if they are linked with a degree of autonomy and choice for children.

If children work only with others of similar attainments then opportunities to see later stages of the learning are missed. A family session in a municipal swimming pool is a good illustration of a mixed attainment group! The pool will probably contain apprehensive non-swimmers, tentative doggy paddlers and efficient freestylers. Many adults state that they learned to swim not by being taught directly but by watching and then trying to imitate swimmers at their local pools. One might argue that they would have learned more efficiently with direct teaching in a group of similar non-swimmers. Both strategies have their place but self-initiated learning in a mixed ability group has the advantage of being paced by the learner and can build confidence not just in the task learned (e.g. swimming) but in the process of being a learner. Swimmers who learned to swim by watching others are often very proud that they taught themselves in this way!

Work groups, which comprise children of varying attainments and incorporate individual choices, encourage children to try out ideas on one another and to extend their learning without necessarily having to go through the teacher to achieve this. This autonomy is important, given that teachers have been found to over-estimate the learning needs of children with learning difficulties and to under-estimate relatively able children (Bennett *et al.* 1984). Mis-matching is likely to be diminished if children have opportunities to develop their own interests within structured guidelines, perhaps (depending partly on age range) contributing to a common goal. Chapter 6 contains examples of topic-based activities in which children of differing attainments could work together. Children with learning difficulties may lack confidence in their abilities and therefore their choices of activities in mixed attainment groups needs to be carefully monitored so that confidence is developed.

Pairs of children working together

Various types of paired learning have been carried out with children with learning difficulties. Peer tutoring (Allen 1976, Topping 1988) is one well-known approach which has, in various guises, been used by teachers of mixed ability classes. Peer tutoring also occurs across classes, so that older children with learning difficulties tutor younger children with lower attainments than themselves. Peer tutoring, or similar types of activity, are a useful means through which children with learning difficulties practise skills that they have already acquired. Peer tutoring may also help the generalisation and application of these skills. These are aspects, as discussed earlier (chapter 3), which are vital in the consolidation of learning and are very important for children with learning difficulties who need regularly to practise generalising and applying skills and knowledge. Some schools have developed 'shared reading' time in which, for a short period, all children in the school are paired and one child reads the book to his or her partner. They then discuss the book and perhaps change roles.

Peer tutoring involves an unequal relationship between the tutor and the tutored, as one child (the tutor) has skills which the tutored child clearly lacks. Some writers (e.g. Glynn 1985) have criticised this approach because the child being tutored is always dependent on the child tutor. This criticism can be avoided if all children have the chance to take on the roles of both tutor and tutored. For example, 7-year olds might be paired every Monday with 9-year olds for tutors and on Thursdays, as tutors themselves , with 5-year olds. A variety of research has shown that even children as young as 4 or 5 are adept at making appropriate adjustments in the way in which they talk to other children, differentiating between able and less able listeners and older or younger children (Wood 1988). These abilities have also been demonstrated by young mainstream children when communicating with classmates with severe learning difficulties (Lewis 1990, Lewis and Carpenter 1990). The 6- and 7-year old mainstream children whom I recorded were skilful in re-phrasing instructions when working with partners with severe learning difficulties. They often shortened an instruction when it seemed not to have been understood. For example, 'Give me that long pencil from the box' was changed to 'Give me that one' (pointing). Vocabulary which was likely to have been difficult to comprehend was also changed. For example, one child said to her partner, 'Colour in the circle' and then changed this to 'Colour in the round'.

A different type of paired learning (sometimes called collaborative learning) occurs when two children of similar attainment levels work together on a problem. The roots for this work are in 'post-Piagetian' studies of young children's cognitive development and the view that cognitive development takes place when one child is challenged cognitively by another. This happens when one child is only slightly more advanced than the other. (The research has been reviewed by David Wood 1988.) It is difficult to apply the research directly to typical classrooms but one important point is that children benefit from having opportunities to work in a *variety* of individual, paired, small group and whole class contexts. A mix of these groupings, used flexibly, is likely to foster both cognitive and social development. Record sheets which show children's experiences of different types of group help to prevent a situation in which, by default rather than planning, children spend much time in individualised work. This applies especially to those who find school-based learning difficult. Unless there is deliberate planning for group work, these children may spend nearly all learning time in carefully planned and appropriate, but ultimately isolating, individualised programmes. This then compounds the difficulties that children with learning difficulties often have in developing social relationships with classmates. (The same difficulty arises in relation to able children given highly individualised work.) The playground may become the only opportunity for group activity.

A SPECIFIC ISSUE CONCERNING GROUPING:

Integrating children from special schools or units into mainstream classes

The points discussed earlier in this chapter apply to working groups which contain children who work part time in the class because they spend part of the time in special schools. However, there are some additional points, which concern integration generally, which can be made in the context of how children are grouped for teaching. Many commentators on the ERA, and the Bill which preceded it, have argued that the integration of children from special into mainstream schools will be threatened by the legislation. At best, the ERA has been seen as doing nothing to strengthen the pro-integration stance of the 1981 Education Act (Wedell 1988). Issues about educational integration need to be seen in the light of the ERA as a whole, as well as in the context of the NC specifically. In relation to the former, opting out procedures, the increased powers given to school governors, and changes in funding arrangements may hamper integration but this is an area about which very little is certain at present.

There are, alongside these concerns, some positive aspects of the NC in relation to integration (this is discussed more fully in Carpenter and Lewis 1989 and Lewis 1991). Importantly, the NC provides a common language for detailed discussion of curricula across mainstream and special schools. The fact that it is common to both sectors will not only help mainstream school teachers to recognise that what happens in special schools is not totally different from what happens in mainstream schools but also help special school teachers to see links between what they do and what is happening in mainstream schools.

The NC also provides a series of common curriculum ladders for all children, whether they are in mainstream or special education settings. The NCC's Circular 5 (1989a) explicitly includes, within the common curricular framework, children with severe or profound and multiple learning difficulties (SLD or PMLD, respectively). This is a radical stance and shows how far thinking about those children's educational needs has come because, until 1970, those children were regarded as coming under the aegis of Health rather than Education authorities. It is interesting that, within the broad context of the NC and children with SEN, some of the fiercest debate has surrounded this issue. Some writers (e.g. Tilstone and Steel 1989) have argued for including in the NC children with SLD or PMLD in order to emphasise the similarities between those and other children. Other writers (e.g. Daniels and Ware 1990, Emblem and Conti-Ramsden 1990) argue that the suitability of the NC for those children is open to serious doubt.

However, if there is integration between special and mainstream schools, and if foundation subjects are the foci of that integration, then it is likely to be helpful if there is a common curricular framework (Lewis 1988). The NC will make it easier to develop continuity and progression across special and mainstream school curricula for individual pupils. The importance of this is illustrated in Neville Bennett and Allyson Cass's (1989) case studies of children transferring from special to mainstream schools. Curriculum continuity was described as poor for three of the five children studied. Problems were particularly acute when the transition was made at mid-secondary, rather than the junior/secondary transfer stage.

The use of NC SOAs to guide curricular decisions across mainstream and special schools is described by Archer (1989). He comments that a teacher from a special school will be able to match the curricular needs of a pupil from the special school with what is offered by the mainstream school (and vice versa). Thus a child from the special school on, say, level 3 of the science curriculum can be placed in a mainstream school class in which level 3 science work will be carried out. However, the possible dangers of imbuing NC levels with spurious accuracy should be borne in mind (see chapter 5).

Children of differing levels can also work together effectively on a common task, drawing on different but complementary skills. This is another application of the paired or mixed attainment work groups that were discussed earlier in the chapter. In one integration project (Carpenter *et al.* 1986, Moore *et al.* 1987), involving 6- and 7-year olds in a first school and peers with severe learning difficulties, staff decided to encourage the children to work cooperatively in pairs comprising a child from the mainstream school and a child from the SLD school. An example of a collaborative activity which has used in this project was wax-resist painting. In this activity the child from the mainstream school wrote his or her name or that of his or her partner in wax on a white sheet of paper. The child from the SLD school then painted over this. It was the responsibility of the mainstream school child to write both children's names on the picture when it was dry. This idea can be applied to tasks within the NC. For example, a game for a pair of children involving the making of 3D shapes from 2D card or plastic shapes could require one child to sort the shapes by colour (Science AT 15, level 1) or by shape (Mathematics AT 10, level 1) and the other child to build the shapes into, for example, pyramids or cubes (Mathematics AT 10, level 4).

This chapter has reviewed various aspects of the NC in relation to the grouping of children at both a broad organisational level of allocating children to classes and work groupings within classes. The tacit and even overt approval given in the NC to collaborative group or paired work is a feature which should work to the benefit of all children.

Chapter 8

Resources

The focus of this chapter is on ways in which we can make the most of resources, both human and material. I start from the premiss that we are not likely to see major increases in funding for staff or materials and that therefore obtaining the maximum benefit from the resources that we do have will be crucial.

RESOURCES: PEOPLE

The first part of the chapter will focus on several connected issues:

- Making the best use of available adults in the classroom,
- The role of a co-ordinator for SEN,
- Staffing for children integrated from special schools,
- Classmates as a resource,
- Care-givers,
- Support services.

Making the best use of available adults in the clasroom

The traditional picture of the class teacher working alone for the whole school week has been gradually eroded. The 1987 primary staffing survey (DES 1988b) found that in England 18 per cent of full-time infant class teachers and 39 per cent of full-time junior class teachers did some teaching of children from other classes. Time spent teaching in other classes was usually brief (between one and three hours in the survey week). Another significant change in primary classrooms over the last decade has been the increase in the range and number of adults in the classroom at any one time. This has led to an expanding of the class teacher's role to encompass not just teaching but also the management of a diverse group of adult helpers. These adults may be involved with children with learning difficulties because class teachers often feel that it is these children who, in particular, need additional adult help.

Adults who work in the classroom alongside the class teacher and who might spend at least part of their time with children with learning difficulties include:

- Peripatetic support teachers for children with learning difficulties,
- Peripatetic support teachers for children for whom English is a second language (some of these children may also have difficulties in learning),
- Bilingual teachers based in the school,
- Curriculum support teachers working to develop school policy in a particular curricular area,
- A school curriculum co-ordinator for a particular curricular area,
- Other teachers in a shared open-plan base,
- Educational psychologists,
- Special needs specialists such as speech therapists,
- Classroom assistants/ancillaries,
- Nursery nurses (NNEBs),
- Pupils from local schools,
- Young people on work experience programmes,
- Higher education students (some of whom may be on teacher training courses, others may be studying for qualifications in parallel fields such as social work or psychology),
- Care-givers (some of whom may be qualified teachers),
- School governors (some of whom may be qualified teachers),
- Visiting teachers from other schools,
- Miscellaneous visitors, some of whom may carry out some teaching (e.g. older people considering training for teaching),
- People on licensed, or articled, teacher schemes.

A first step in co-ordinating the contributions of this diverse group of people is to establish the particular strengths of these individuals (e.g. music, technology), so that these can be utilised to complement the work of the class teacher. Next, it is useful to identify which of these people will work regularly, and which irregularly, with the class. This will influence the types of activities and roles which the class teacher plans for and with these adults. It is crucial that the class teacher (or one specific class teacher, if teachers are working in a collaborative team) retains overall responsibility for co-ordinating the work of individual children with difficulties in learning. Such a task can be very time-consuming so, and ideally, primary teachers should have time away from teaching to carry out this role.

Although there are potential advantages in having a number of adults with a class, there are also possible difficulties. These include conflicts between the adults, confusion for children because conflicting information is given by different adults, children 'playing off' one adult against another, uncertainty about individual adult's roles, and a feeling by some adults that they are not wanted/needed. Time spent with children may be replaced by time spent organising adults and this may be unsatisfying for the teacher. Thus, initial enthusiasm for co-teaching may pall as the associated demands for sustained communication between the adults are not met.

There are also issues concerning relationships between care-givers who work in the classroom and care-givers of children in the class. Kath Beck (1989) has discussed some of the dilemmas which can arise. She quotes a parent who expressed suspicion about confidentiality: 'Is a problem about my child discussed between a helper-parent and teacher?' (Beck 1989: 11). Another parent reported some grounds for this type of concern: 'There was an incident recently where one lady was discussing the skills, and the lack of them, of the children she had worked with. It was very unfair on the children, who were doing so well. Several mothers heard this and were quite annoyed, which is understandable' (Beck 1989: 12). All classroom helpers and teachers should be aware of this issue and be alerted to the need to avoid passing on judgements about children, staff or other care-givers.

Regular adult co-teachers

The increase in the number of adults working in classrooms plus accumulating evidence of the amount of time which primary teachers spend within the classroom on administrative tasks point to the need to rationalise tasks allocated to adults in the classroom. One way in which to co-ordinate the work of teams of adults is to assign specific roles to each co-teacher. (I am using the term 'co-teacher' for any adult, not necessarily formally qualified as a teacher, who works in the class as a teacher.)

Judith McBrien and Jane Weightman (1980) and Gary Thomas (1988) have described a useful way of planning for groups of adults to work together in a classroom. They have identified three specific roles which might be taken by the adults. These roles are: an 'individual helper', an 'activity manager', and a 'mover'. Gary Thomas (1988) focuses on an 'activity period' in which adults are allocated these specific roles. It would be feasible to apply these, for example, to an afternoon in which several adults regularly worked with one class. The individual helper(s) works with a succession of children, giving specific and detailed individual teaching. The activity manager(s) looks after the rest of the children in the class. Ideally, these children should be working on activities to which they have already been introduced. In terms of the model (Haring *et al.* 1978) discussed in chapter 3, the children should be at fluency, generalisation or adaptation levels of learning in these activities. The mover(s) aims to maintain the flow of activity in the class by dealing with minor distractions, such as a note brought in from another teacher, a child who feels ill, or pencils needing to be sharpened.

This approach has wide application in that these three basic roles could be taken by a range of adults. Some of the 'mover' role might be taken by children. The system is adaptable and could suit different classes so that in a particular class the teacher could plan to have certain sessions in which there are, for example, two individual helpers, one activity manager and one mover. This type of systematic allocation of roles could go a long way towards resolving some of the potential difficulties of several adults working as co-teachers in a class. It would still be important for the class teacher to co-ordinate, explain and take responsibility for the system.

Irregular adult co-teachers

The approach described above is appropriate if individual helpers come regularly. It is less feasible if help is erratic and individuals rarely work regularly in one class. Then, a more useful approach may be to focus on a development of the individual helper role. Some schools have developed individual 'task cards' or 'day books' for children, in which their work for the day, or perhaps work for

a specific curricular area, is given. This enables any adult helping
in the classroom to pick up the card or book and know immediately on which learning targets or activities a child is working. Figure
8.1 shows the type of task card which could be designed for a child
in a primary school class. The card could be filled in by the class
teacher each week and placed in a folder which is open to all adult
helpers. There might be several children in the class for whom the
teacher maintains this system.

The approach has worked well in a range of schools. In some,
the cards or books were kept by the children, rather than centrally
by the class teacher, and co-teachers talked to the child about
selected areas for extra help. In either case, adult helpers have
specific foci for their help and feel that they are fulfilling a useful
role. They get to know well the individuals with whom they are

Figure 8.1 Task card for Richard

RICHARD   Date: Week beginning 4 February

Handwriting is the main focus for additional help this week. Please
check that 'o' and 'u' are being written in correct direction. Also pencil
grip is poor: needs lots of practice in correct pencil hold and position
when writing. Develop flowing writing movements with variety of
pencils/pens.

Maths: developing work on number patterns. Understands the 2, 5
and 10 patterns. Needs help with '3', started this last week but still
very unsure. Go on to 6 and 9 after this. Check that he understands
by using blocks.

Language/literacy: making a book about insects. Has interviewed all
the children in the class about their favourite/disliked insects, part
way through block graphs to show the results. Headings for graphs
needed. Also some discussion about how to interpret the block
graphs. Wants to write a story about an ant in a jam factory, needs
help with individual words for this. Encourage him to use a picture
dictionary and the word lists around the class to help with these.

Finished last reading book. Encourage free choice from blue box in
book box system (i.e. at a parallel level to the book just finished).

(Science: joining in group project on local woodland. Next activity will
be to make detailed observational drawings of a 1-metre square
patch.)

working and the children, for their part, enjoy the 'special' help. This is co-ordinated by the class teacher who amends the cards or books as necessary.

If the picture presented here is of the burden of working with, and organising, other adults in the classroom, then it is important to stress also the benefits of working alongside other adults. Jenny Nias's (1989) work on teachers starting teaching is very illuminating and illustrates how supportive such adult co-teachers can be. Nearly half of the young teachers in her research attributed their survival in their first posts to help from one or more specific colleagues. The adults who gave help were not necessarily teachers; classroom assistants, for example, were reported as being very valuable in helping the probationary teacher to 'learn the ropes'.

The role of a co-ordinator for SEN

The school co-ordinator for special needs should be a key person in helping all staff to make the most of opportunities for children's learning. The findings of the Primary survey (DES 1978b) gave impetus to the trend for school-based curriculum co-ordinators (or consultants) in all aspects of the curriculum. This survey found that, at its best, a good co-ordinator could do much to promote good practice within the whole school. The development of the role of curriculum co-ordinator was widely advocated (e.g. ILEA 1985b) and successive surveys have shown increased use of curriculum co-ordinators, including those for SEN. An HMI survey of children with SEN in 55 primary and 42 secondary schools (HMI 1989b) concluded that designated specialist co-ordinators for SEN were important contributors in almost all of the schools in which good practice was observed.

It is not possible to make direct comparisons between successive surveys if sampling methods differ. However, there does appear to have been a significant increase in the proportion of schools with an SEN co-ordinator. Approximately one-third of schools (38 per cent) in the 1978 Primary survey had a post of special responsibility for 'remedial work'. Ten years later, a survey by HMI (HMI 1989b) found that two-thirds of the primary schools visited had a designated member of staff with co-ordinating responsibility for children with SEN. Such overall figures mask differences between LEAs and there is wide variation between LEAs concerning co-ordinators for SEN in individual schools. In some LEAs every primary school has a named teacher as the SEN co-ordinator. In some schools this is a scale post; in others, responsibility for SEN has been added to a curricular area, for example, language. There are considerable disadvantages if responsibility for SEN is marginalised in any way. This may be reflected by a part-time teacher having responsibility for SEN, by the lack of an incentive allowance for SEN, or by an allowance which is lower than allowances for, say, science or English.

The 1987 primary staffing surveys (DES 1988b, WO 1988) collated a wide range of data about teachers' qualifications, experience and positions in primary schools. Only a small proportion of full-time primary teachers in England and Wales (3 and 6 per cent respectively) had qualifications in teaching children with special needs. Qualifications were defined very broadly. In England, approximately one-third of these qualifications were SEN as a first or second subject at degree or certificate of education levels; the remainder were mainly qualifications from short-term courses, or SEN as part of a PGCE course. (Comparable figures for Wales were presented differently.) Special responsibility for SEN was held by a much wider group of teachers than just those with SEN qualifications. Approximately 90 per cent of the full-time primary teachers in England with 'SEN leadership responsibility' had no qualifications in SEN. The data are presented for teachers as a group so it is, unfortunately, not possible to know the proportion of schools in the survey which had a teacher with an SEN responsibility. About half of the full-time teachers in England with leadership responsibilities for SEN did no specialist 'SEN' teaching. For the other teachers, there was a wide spread in terms of the amount of time spent teaching only children with SEN (ranging from one hour to over sixteen hours per week). Data are not given for the amount of time spent working alongside other teachers.

In some schools, the term 'special needs co-ordinator' has been replaced by 'learning support teacher' and Alan Dyson (1990) has advocated changing the term and role to 'effective learning consultant'. The newer terms reflect the emphasis outlined in chapter 1, that all teachers should be trying to help all of their pupils to learn as effectively as possible. Children with particular difficulties in learning are one aspect of this approach. While the rationale behind the use of new terms and roles for the special needs co-ordinator is to be applauded, such a change may lead to difficulties in monitoring what is happening to posts for SEN. These posts may, in any case, be jeopardised by the subject-based approach of the NC, which is likely to lead to greater emphasis on subject co-ordinators at the expense of broader based posts, whether these are labelled 'effective learning' or 'special needs'.

A review of job specifications, HMI reports and discussion by commentators suggests that the roles of a co-ordinator for SEN might include:

- Monitoring and reviewing curricula of individual children. In the context of the NC this may encompass helping staff to differentiate the NC in appropriate ways.
- Planning how SATs might be carried out with children with particular difficulties so that the children work as well as possible and are not upset by tasks which are beyond them.
- Co-ordinating work within the school for the full range of children with SEN, including any partial integration programmes.
- Leading revision of relevant school policy.
- Advising colleagues on particular SEN approaches and techniques.
- Teaching children with SEN in collaboration with the class teacher. This may be one of the more daunting aspects of the role. Viv King (1989) has outlined various ways in which teachers might work collaboratively within the classroom. These include: one teacher leading and one supporting, the class working in mixed ability groups and both teachers circulating, either teacher targeting particular pupils, halving the class and working 'in tandem', one teaching and one observing/assessing, and a 'double act' in which the two teachers work conjointly.
- Attending and reporting back on SEN courses and workshops.
- Knowing and understanding the statutory aspects of the ERA in relation to children with SEN.
- Liaising with care-givers and outside agencies working with children with SEN.
- Giving talks to governors and keeping them informed about work relating to children with SEN.
- Providing governors with detailed information about the range of support services needed by and/or available to the

school. The extension of governors' powers to include budgeting makes this important, as provision for children with SEN is often a very expensive item for, perhaps, relatively few children. (This topic is discussed more fully in the 1989 ACE bulletin 32 and the 1990 ACE/AGIT conference report.)

• Becoming increasingly involved in obtaining additional resources from voluntary agencies, given the changes in school funding arrangements. This has happened for some LEA support services and they have obtained grants from national 'Children in Need' appeals. This does raise political issues about whether or not it is right to draw on money from charities to help fund a state education system.

The above list is a very extensive set of responsibilities and, it may be argued, rather unrealistic. Such a role would be impossible if tied to full-time class teaching. HMI's survey of children with statements of SEN in mainstream schools noted that, where the SEN postholders were allocated time to pursue their duties (such as advising and supporting colleagues and organising identification, assessment and review procedures), 'it was possible for pupils and staff to be effectively supported, good practice disseminated and school procedures established and followed' (HMI 1990c: para. 32). Some governing bodies may be sufficiently sensitive to special needs issues to create a post in which these can be developed alongside, say, a half-teaching timetable.

Staffing for children integrated from special schools

A specific aspect of staffing for children with difficulties in school-based learning concerns children who have statements of SEN under the 1981 Education Act. By definition, these children have learning difficulties which require special provision to be made for them. Children with statements in mainstream schools might be registered full-time in the mainstream school or might be on the register of a special school or unit and attend a mainstream school for part of the school week. I shall describe the latter as 'child-based link schemes' to distinguish them from 'adult-based link schemes' in which it is staff rather than pupils who move between special and mainstream schools.

The pattern of statementing and provision for children with statements varies enormously across different LEAs. Evidence about the extent of this variation is provided by the House of Commons Select Committee which investigated the working of the 1981 Education Act (House of Commons 1987), research into the implementation of the Act (Goacher *et al.* 1988) and data collection about integration (Swann 1989). Brian Goacher and his colleagues (1988) found that the percentage of statemented children in individual LEAs who were attending mainstream schools ranged from below 10 per cent to over 23 per cent. More specifically, but from data collected at a similar period, the House of Commons Select Committee (1987) report comparable figures for each LEA. The percentage of pupils with statements placed in mainstream schools varied from 69 per cent (Cornwall) to 2 per cent (Manchester). These figures may be misleading and may over-estimate the percentages of children with statements in mainstream schools, as, four years later, it was being reported that many children in special schools had still not been given statements of SEN (Mittler 1990). If new statements are given to children attending mainstream schools while children continuing in special schools are not given statements, then proportions are distorted.

Overall, there has been a trend towards the integration of children with statements into mainstream schools but this is much stronger in some areas than in others and for some groups of children. Children with sensory impairments have been more likely than other groups of statemented children to be integrated into mainstream schools and more likely to receive appropriately differentiated curricula (HMI 1990c). It is too soon to be clear about the impact of the ERA on statementing policies but there is evidence (see chapter 10) of an increase in the numbers of children being given statements of SEN.

Discussion of placements in special or mainstream schools overlooks a shift towards increasing child-based link schemes. These are hidden when data report only schools in which children are nominally registered. The NFER research into links between mainstream and special schools (Jowett *et al.* 1988) found that link schemes were widespread. Brian Goacher and his co-workers (1988) also found that most special school heads reported increased links with mainstream schools. There has been much debate about the rationale and effectiveness of child-based link schemes. The Select Committee on the working of the 1981 Act (House of Commons 1987) took the view that link schemes are an important aspect of integration. Whether special school, main-stream school or some child-based link scheme between the two is the best option for a child and his or her family will depend on a range of factors, including staff attitudes and resources. Some writers (e.g. Moore and Morrison 1988) argue that advocates of child-based link schemes are taking a weak view of integration and that the special school children are always visitors, rather than genuine classmates, in the mainstream school. As such, child-based link schemes constitutute only partial integration and sustain, rather than diminish, segregation.

Some LEAs have made extra staffing available to foster educational integration. This has taken various forms, including an integration support teacher who accompanies groups or individual children from a special to a mainstream school, who gives advice to the mainstream school and/or teaches collaboratively with mainstream school teachers. (See Carpenter *et al.* 1988 for a fuller discussion of the role of an integration support teacher.) Classroom ancillaries may be provided to help children with particular needs, for example, arising from physical disabilities. In recent DES documents, these personnel are referred to as 'SSAs': special support assistants.

The DES draft Circular on staffing for pupils with special educational needs (DES 1990e) is very tentative about fixing staffing levels. It is described as a 'broad guide for planning purposes' rather than a 'blueprint' (para. 4) and there is no commitment to provide funding to ensure that the recommended staffing levels are met. Recommended levels of staffing for children with SEN who are integrated into mainstream schools are vague:

> It is imposible to stipulate an appropriate level of provision for SSAs [special support assistants] to meet the needs of pupils with statements placed individually in ordinary schools... It is probable that many pupils in bands 2–4* will require some SSA support when placed in an ordinary school, but this will not always be the case.
>
> (DES 1990e: Annex B, para. 10)

* Band 1: children with profound and multiple learning difficulties (PMLD),
  Band 2: children with severe communication difficulties,
  Band 3: children with severe emotional and behavioural difficulties,
  Band 4: children with severe developmental difficulties,
  Band 5: children with 'other learning difficulties'.

There is no firm commitment to provide additional staffing or to encourage a flexible response to determining staffing needs in order to foster educational integration. Evidence from experiences of integration suggests that extra staffing may be needed initially, especially when the children to be integrated have severe learning or emotional difficulties. This extra staffing may be needed to prepare mainstream school staff rather than for the direct support of children with SEN. In the longer term, such additional staffing can often be decreased as mainstream school teachers gain confidence and expertise. 'Band 1' children (with profound and multiple learning difficulties) are presumably not anticipated to be integrated into mainstream schools, although there has been some work in this area. The draft Circular also leaves open the question of what might be needed by children in band 5 ('other learning difficulties'). Their exclusion from the second sentence in the above extract implies that no additional staffing is envisaged for their integration. The draft Circular does not make specific recommendations about either staffing levels for non-statemented children with special needs or meeting the complexities of staffing in a special school which is involved in a variety of link schemes.

The document stresses the need for provision to lead to more cost-effective use of staff and other resources in order to meet the needs of pupils with SEN, whether the children are in special or mainstream schools. It calls for flexibility of staffing, such as teachers from special schools working in mainstream schools, and vice versa. It is suggested that teachers from mainstream schools might work in special schools 'to ensure delivery of a balanced and broadly based curriculum' (DES 1990e: Annex B, para. 3) while staffing in special schools might need to be increased if special schools act as resource centres or make regular contributions to mainstream schools. How the financial aspects might be managed if the mainstream but not the special school is operating LMS is not clear.

More generally, where specific additional help is provided for children with learning difficulties in mainstream schools, there may be issues about whether the individual adult(s) works only with the statemented child or with a range of children. This raises complex issues and has, in some instances, led to complaints by the child's care-givers that the terms of the statement are not being met because specific additional help (e.g. three hours per week for

individualised programmes) is not being given. The closer and
better the relationship between the school and the care-givers, the
less likely it is that such an issue will arise. If a child with, for
example, severe learning difficulties, has an SSA for, say, ten hours
per week (two hours each morning), then, unless it is clearly
specified in the statement, the class teacher (in discussion with
others) will have to decide what is the best use of that help. It may
be totally within the classroom and with that child alone, it may be
within the classroom with a small group including that child, or it
may be with the child in a withdrawal group for specialised
teaching. (See chapter 7 for discussion about withdrawal group
work.) It seems reasonable for the special helper to work with
other children while the class teacher works with the statemented
child. This would also help to avoid a sense of over-possessiveness
between the statemented child and the SSA, leading to covert
segregation within the classroom.

The issues are not just about the amount of individualised
teaching but also about the quality of the teaching received by
children with learning difficulties. The need for mainstream
school teachers to receive advice about teaching children with
severe learning difficulties is evident from HMI's survey of 43
primary phase schools attended by a range of children with
statements of special educational needs (HMI 1990c). This survey
found that there was wide variation in the effectiveness of mainstream school placements for statemented children but that, in
general, children with sensory impairments or speech and language difficulties received work which was better matched to their
needs than did children with severe learning difficulties. The
survey found that additional teaching support was sometimes provided by classroom ancillaries. These people had had no in-service
training in the role and 'There was evidence that a lack of
knowledge and skill could result in inappropriate intervention in
activities thus inhibiting pupils' progress' (HMI 1990c: para. 37).
It is clearly crucial that all staff, including classroom assistants,
SSAs and nursery nurses working in the classroom, are included in
in-service training. At present, it is not clear whether child-based
link schemes will continue in the light of LMS, formula funding
and the implementation of the NC. Link schemes have often
arisen from contacts between individual heads and teachers,
rather than from LEA policy. This may make them more rather
than less secure, if the ERA leads to a strengthening of

school-based decision making. The future position is uncertain concerning adult support staff for children with difficulties in learning, whether with or without statements. However, there will continue to be potential support from other children in the class.

Classmates as a resource

Classmates are a potential resource for all children. If the classroom climate is one in which children are encouraged to work together, then one child helping another child with, for example, spellings is not conspicuous. Thus a child with learning difficulties being taught by another child is just a natural part of the classroom ethos. Similarly, if it is recognised that all children can give and receive help in different ways and for different tasks then children with difficulties in learning are likely to experience both sides of this. As discussed in chapter 7 in relation to pupil grouping, it is important that they do experience both the giving and receiving of help.

There are several ways in which, within the classroom, this type of strategy can be encouraged. For example, some teachers have a 'rule' that children always ask one another for help before they ask an adult. The sharing and reporting back of work is a common practice in many primary schools and encourages children to be positive about what other children have done. The mutual support provided is especially important for children who, through repeated difficulties in school tasks, may have become apprehensive about revealing their work to other children. Many schools have fostered shared learning in which children work together on a task. This can be developed so that children produce materials, such as stories, for other classes or other schools. 'Round robin' stories, in which successive classes or schools add to a continuing story, have become popular. Some schools have developed desk top publishing ventures, enabling the final class or school to reproduce the story/newspaper for all of the children, classes or schools involved. Gerda Hanko (1985), Steven Bossert (1987), Sarah Tann (1988) and John Thacker (1990) have all discussed group learning in classrooms and they provide useful analyses.

Care-givers

The importance of liaison with care-givers was discussed in chapter

4 in relation to identifying where children are in their learning. The ways in which care-givers might work within the classroom has been discussed earlier in this chapter but not all care-givers are able or willing to work in the school. Much of children's learning is stimulated by what happens at home and, generally, schools now work hard at developing and sustaining links between home and school. This may be done both for educational reasons, such as enhancing children's reading through various 'home reading' schemes; and for political reasons because a variety of legislation (notably the 1986 and 1988 Education Acts) has given care-givers and school governors greater power and influence over what happens in schools.

There have been many imaginative schemes to develop home–school links (see Wolfendale 1983, Topping and Wolfendale 1985, Widlake 1986, Bastiani 1987). In the present context, attention is specifically on ways in which care-givers can help to develop the learning of children who find school tasks difficult. An important aspect is sustaining the child's motivation for learning. This is a two-way process; the school may explicitly develop interests begun at home and the home may extend school-based learning. The range of activities which children carry out with care-givers, siblings, other family members or friends can be a rich basis for applying and generalising skills and knowledge. If teachers do not see care-givers, then informal notebooks between home and school help to sustain two-way communication. This is especially important if the child is unable or unwilling to talk to care-givers or teachers about what he or she has done at school or home.

Gerda Hanko (1985) has written of the specific issues surrounding collaboration with care-givers of children who have difficulties in school-based learning. School staff may feel wary about collaboration because they anticipate that care-givers will attribute the child's difficulties to poor teaching. Discussing this openly means that teachers may have to face searching questions about what and how they have been teaching. Requirements to report to care-givers on children's progress on NC ATs may increase this. Research into the progress of children through infant schools (Tizard *et al* 1988) found that the teachers rarely explained teaching methods to care-givers. Care-givers may have different ideas from the school about the best way of helping a child with difficulties. One parent commented, 'I want to work with the school but I don't like it that he's treated differently from the others, I don't like it that he has his own special desk' (Sedgwick 1989: 127). Meanwhile, the care-givers may fear that they will be seen as the problem and blamed for the child's difficulties. There are grounds for these fears. Paul Croll and Diana Moses (1985) asked 428 junior school teachers about hypothesised causes of difficulties in learning. Home factors were thought to be the cause of slow learning or poor reading for one-third of these children. Home factors were given as the cause of emotional or behavioural difficulties for approximately two-thirds of children with these problems. Home factors may be a contributing cause of difficulties but are outside the teacher's control. Genuinely collaborative home–school relations will help to diminish negative stereotyping of care-givers of children with difficulties in learning and to foster joint planning of constructive strategies.

Support services

There is a wide range of support services available to teachers. Many of these include a concern with promoting educational opportunities for children with learning difficulties. In most LEAs these support services have included: school psychological service (sometimes still known as a child guidance clinic), school health service, speech therapists, education welfare service, peripatetic support teachers ('remedial service'), special school outreach workers, inspectors/advisers with responsibility for children with SEN, professional development centres and curriculum support teams. Some of these services have different names in various LEAs. For example, Caroline Gipps and her co-workers (1987) found 35 alternative names in use for 'peripatetic remedial services'!

In addition, a range of support services (such as medical, social and/or psychiatric) is directed to individual children. There is also a wide range of national groups, mainly voluntary, which provide information, advice and materials concerned with the education of children with specific difficulties. (See Male and Thompson 1985, Darnbrough and Kinrade 1985, Leclerc 1985, and TIPS [Dawson 1985] for details about many of these groups.)

The Cox Report (DES/WO 1989c), containing proposals for the curriculum for English, endorsed the value of the support services:

Some pupils with SEN ... may need assistance to enable them to communicate their achievements .... For example, speech therapists, ... medical specialists or psychologists. We recognise that there may be resource implications, but feel the involvement of such specialists to be essential if the pupils concerned are to be enabled to perform in English to their full potential.

(DES/WO 1989c: para. 12.16)

HMI (1989c) surveyed support services for children with SEN and concluded that service provision did make a difference to the schools and pupils who received support. HMI found that most schools would not have been able to bring together the range of expertise and resources that was evident in the majority of the support services which HMI visited.

It is not clear what the impact of LMS and formula funding will be on support services. At the time of writing, most of the educational support services will continue to be funded from discretionary exceptions in local authority budgets. Some slimming down seems inevitable and, in time, schools will probably have to buy in at least some of the services. Those services will be pushed into producing menus of what will be available at various prices. How this works may depend in part on whether or not the children to be served by the service have statements of SEN. The statement could serve as a guarantee of resources which would otherwise be perceived by school governors as too costly and/or unnecessary.

RESOURCES: MATERIALS

The second part of this chapter considers the material resources available to help a teacher to provide children with suitable opportunities for learning. Two aspects are considered: first, briefly, the variety of materials available and, second, a way of organising and co-ordinating some of these resources.

Range of available resources

Local support services, such as those listed above, may loan materials as well as, or instead of, people to foster the educational opportunities of children with learning difficulties. In particular, special school outreach services and peripatetic support services for children with learning difficulties have, since the ERA, been producing curricular analyses of ways in which POSs might be made accessible to children with learning difficulties. At the time of writing, much of this material is still in draft or pilot form but it is probable that a wide range of such materials will be available over the next few years. Such curricular outlines may well be followed up with packages or examples of classroom-based resources. The impact of LMS may be to encourage schools and services to sell such packages to receiving schools.

Professional bodies for teachers concerned about children with learning difficulties provide advice and, in many cases, publish relevant materials (see Leclerc 1985, appendix B). In addition, the national bodies referred to under support services sometimes have specific resources available.

Co-ordinating materials

Eldridge Cleaver said, 'There is no more neutrality in the world, you either have to be part of the solution or you're going to be part of the problem – there ain't no middle ground.' One way in which teachers in primary schools can be 'part of the solution' in helping children who find school-based learning difficult is through the effective organisation of relevant resources. This section describes an approach to co-ordinating resources, for children with learning difficulties in primary schools, in ways which are consistent with the demands of the NC.

The class teacher may be on the receiving end of a great variety of materials in connection with enhancing educational opportunities for children with learning difficulties. The approach described here is one way in which different materials could be combined into a single, co-ordinated and coherent system. It could be incorporated into different types of classroom organisa- tion, including subject-based or cross-curricular, whether organised around individuals, 'mixed ability', or 'similar ability' groupings. The ways in which resources are organised do not dictate methods of learning but they should enhance the opportunities for learning, whatever the teaching style. The approach has been used widely in a variety of primary and special education settings. It aims to make good use of the time and resources available without isolating children with learning dif- ficulties from their classmates. The approach also reflects the need for both structure in children's learning and breadth of teaching methods.

Research into the effectiveness of different teaching styles and surveys by HMI about successful classroom practise repeatedly emphasise the importance of a variety of teaching methods in promoting children's learning. This has been discussed in chapter 6 and is mentioned here in order to put into context the approach described for co-ordinating classroom materials. It is a system which lends itself to relatively narrow and specific skills. Much classroom learning is not of this type, but some is, and for those areas it is a useful approach. Phonics, handwriting, spelling and some number skills are particularly appropriate foci of this very structured approach. However, all of these need to be supplemented with broader-based approaches.

Opportunities for learning are enhanced if the relevant resources are clearly organised and accessible to children. At a basic level this means having routine classroom materials, such as scissors and paper, clearly labelled with pictures as well as written notices to show what goes where in the classroom. At another level, learning materials also need to be clearly organised. This is not a problem if all, for example, mathematics work is done from one central scheme but, as the diversity of materials and teaching methods increases, classroom organisation becomes a critical factor in promoting or limiting learning. I have discussed the possible range of adults in the classroom who may need to draw on a common pool of resources for work with children with learning difficulties. A good test of the clarity and coherence of the way in which learning materials are organised is to ask: if a supply teacher were to take over the class, would he or she be able to find, quickly, appropriate learning materials for children with (e.g.) spelling difficulties? This is a reasonable question to ask. The HMI survey of children with SEN in mainstream schools (HMI 1989b) found that, in 18 per cent of the primary schools surveyed, pupils with SEN were being taught by supply or temporary teachers on the day that HMI visited. The primary staffing surveys (DES 1988b, WO 1988), carried out in March 1987, found substantial numbers of staff absent. In England and Wales approximately half of the schools surveyed (58 per cent and 46 per cent respectively) had staff away during the survey week. Supply teachers were used extensively to cover for these absent staff (64 per cent of all absences in England and 41 per cent in Wales). This snapshot does not show the picture over time but recently in-service training linked to the NC, as well as usual absences through sickness, is likely to have increased the use of supply and temporary staff.

All children need regular teachers with whom they can build up warm and positive relationships but this need is particularly important for children with learning difficulties who, as discussed in chapter 3, often lack confidence in learning and find it very difficult to generalise skills and knowledge from one context to another. For children who find school-based learning difficult, a succession of teachers presenting slightly different ways of, for example, setting out and carrying out vertical addition sums can limit progress because the children fail to make links across the different strategies.

A second test of the organisation of materials for children with learning difficulties is to consider to what extent the children are able to find appropriate materials for themselves. If children can find their own learning resources then they can take some control of their own learning, instead of being dependent on the class teacher. Children with difficulties in learning have often had relatively little autonomy because their apparent need for help has been seen as evidence that more, not less, teacher direction is needed. Thus, while other children choose project work topics or reading materials from a broad range, children thought to have learning difficulties have a much narrower choice or even no choice at all. There is an intrinsic dilemma. To give freedom of choice of learning materials may be to permit, perhaps encourage, inappropriate choices which will in the end be counter-productive. If 'free choice' leads to a child opting for relatively easy materials then the activity will not move on the child in his or her learning. If relatively difficult materials are chosen then confidence may be lost and learning does not progress. The skill is to provide choice within a structured framework so that genuine choice is possible but leads to an activity which matches the child's learning needs.

The first stage in organising resources is to find (or write) the outline of the school's curriculum (schemes of work) and any work outside the NC. Parts of these schemes may need to be sub-divided into smaller steps (see chapter 5). This division into smaller steps is the second stage in co-ordinating resources. The nature of the steps will depend on the curricular area. Some skills lend themselves to a hierarchical sequence (e.g. addition of numbers) but other areas of skill or knowledge (e.g. developing creative writing) can only be divided tentatively into wider areas of progression towards the learning target. Ideally the staff in a school should work together to decide on which areas to focus for sub-dividing. The choice will depend on the priorities of the school and its community. Many staff will probably want to begin by sub-dividing early aspects of the core subjects, perhaps science in particular if this has not been developed in the school. The initial division will probably be quite crude, perhaps using ideas such as those in *A Curriculum for All* (NCC 1989d) or in chapter 5 here as starting points. Magazines such as *Special Children* and *Support for Learning* have also contained articles outlining possible sub-divisions. Locally, support services may give advice and perhaps possible ways of sub-dividing parts of the POSs which are relevant to the school's schemes. Some special schools for children with moderate learning difficulties are beginning to make this type of advice available to local mainstream schools.

In many schools, sound–letter links ('phonics') has been an area in which children with difficulties in reading have been given specific and detailed help. This aspect of the curriculum lends itself readily to the approach described here, which would need to be used alongside broader approaches to developing reading. Books such as the NARE *Classroom Index of Phonic Resources* (Herbert and Davies-Jones 1984) provide a breakdown (58 steps) of phonic skills. These 58 steps are not necessarily sequential although they form a broad progression from auditory discrimination to multi-syllabic words. These steps fit well with the broader levels identified in English for key stages 1 and 2 and specifically with levels in AT 4, spelling (DES/WO 1990b).

Having identified aspects of the school's schemes which have been sub-divided into smaller steps suitable for children with learning difficulties, the next stage is to link materials with each step in the curriculum. This stage is likely to involve considerable discussions among staff about the suitability of materials. The NARE *Classroom Index of Phonics Resources* cross-references a wide range of resources for each of the steps identified. It is useful to extract names of materials found within the school and to compile a class or school index of resources. Materials lost or later regarded as inappropriate can be deleted and later additions can be included as they are found or made. The pages can be kept in a binder with a removable plastic spine so that individual sheets can be rewritten if necessary. The phonics teaching should be carried out alongside other work to develop reading and writing. This example relates to phonics but the approach is applicable across a wide range of curricular areas (see Lewis 1983, Turnbull 1981 for application to mathematics).

Each step in the school's scheme needs to have some type of simple coding which can be cross-referenced with relevant materials. This could be done in the same way in which books have been grouped in a 'book box' system, whereby books with similar reading ages are grouped togther and a child chooses a book from a particular level rather than working through one specific scheme.

The clear organisation of resources, which are allied to steps in the curriculum, enables the learner to find materials independently of the teacher. This encourages children's autonomy and allows the teacher to teach rather than to manage resources. The children who will themselves be using the system will often have good ideas about how it should be organised. It is important that a wide variety of types of materials is included at each step, as, otherwise, a child might use specific, narrow approaches to the exclusion of other materials. It is not the aim of this co-ordination of resources to have children working tediously through masses of arid materials! For example, early addition might be developed through: micro-computer programs (individual or group), maths games (individual or group), taped exercises or games (individual or group), games/activities using other audio-visual material (e.g. synchrofax, *Language Master*), workcards, worksheets, and book extracts from various schemes (if necessary cut up so that only work of a similar level and focus is on one card/sheet). All of these could be coded to link with the appropriate step in the school's scheme and place in the NC. A page on early addition in the resource book could list all of these materials and/or the materials could be grouped together physically.

The materials might be stored in one central place in the school so as to be shared by all classes or, depending on the numbers of children to be using the system and/or on the geography of the school, the materials might be shared by only a few classes. The storage area could be relatively large, for example, a converted cloakroom space, or something more modest, such as a filing cabinet or trolley, depending on what is feasible and realistic for the school. Resource banks which are not in a classroom might need to be monitored for part of the time by an adult. However, in schools which have developed this system, an adult has been needed only to monitor the use of the resource bank in the early stages, as the children have quickly become used to the system and been able to use it responsibly and independently. The retrieval of materials from the resource bank is a useful skill for children to acquire and this type of activity is explicitly included in the POS for Reading, key stage 2: 'Pupils should be taught how to use lists of contents, indexes, data bases, a library classification system and catalogues to select information' (DES/WO 1990b: para. 12).

When resources have been grouped and linked with specific parts of the curriculum then gaps may become apparent. Supplementary materials can be produced to fill these gaps. For example, it might become apparent that whereas there is much material on 'magic e', there is very little material to help children's recognition of 'silent letters'. Similarly, if the approach includes materials relating to science, some topics (e.g. 'weather') may be included in a comprehensive and detailed way while there is no breakdown of, for example, how to help children to understand the idea of forces in science. Supplementary materials might be very specific and might need to be made by people working in the school, perhaps using some of the adult helpers identified earlier in this chapter. Other materials might be obtained from the local support services.

This approach to organising and co-ordinating resources has several advantages. Single copies of incomplete sets of materials, which are of little value on their own, can be incorporated into a larger system. Inspection copies, review copies, and home-made materials can all go into the 'bank'. Teachers often make small sets of workcards or have ideas for games for children having specific difficulties, for example, to help a left-handed child with writing, or to help a child to learn a set of sight vocabulary words. Concrete materials might be made to help a child to grasp concepts about, for example, place value or word 'families'. These sets of materials are often not used again and the work is lost. If they slot into a coherent system then they can remain useful and accessible. Children who like learning through a particular medium are able to use their preferred approach as much as possible while still focusing on a learning task which is appropriate for them. Most importantly, children have access to a wide range of materials in learning an area, so that they do not have to keep using the same materials with which they have already failed to learn. Whole staff discussions about co-ordinating resources are important because they help the staff to gain ownership of the system of resources. An imported package might be easier and quicker but it is less likely to be used or to be used effectively.

One danger in the cross-referencing of materials as described here is the possible confusion, for children with learning difficulties, arising from the use of different conventions in materials from different sources. Different print styles are a notorious stumbling block for children just beginning to interpret print. Similarly, terms might not be interpreted as synonymous (e.g. 'add', 'add on', 'go on', 'increase', 'go up', 'add up', 'move on', etc.). Teachers, parents and others involved in compiling resource banks need to look out for, and exclude, materials which use styles, terms, or notations which conflict with those of the school (e.g. a French '7' in mathematics materials). Some schools have sheets of 'agreed' number/letter symbols, and terms (e.g. 'multiply' rather than 'times'), so that all staff explicitly use the same style. This helps to avoid children mis-reading or mis-writing, for example, 3 and 5; 4 and 9; or L/I and 1.

The emphasis on progression and continuity in the NC should minimise unnecessary repetition of the early stages of learning for children with difficulties. Teachers are generally quite good at identifying broadly which children find school-based learning difficult. This needs to be refined so that individual children are matched with appropriate learning experiences for particular curriculum steps. This is important, as inappropriate materials lead the child (or any learner!) to feel frustrated and unmotivated. When the available materials have been co-ordinated in this way, the teacher might decide to add some way of identifying at which point the child is in relation to the particular steps. This relates to many of the points discussed in chapter 4 but in the present context some specific 'game' cards might be made to assess individual steps. This approach is one way in which teachers in primary schools could organise learning materials to meet the needs of children with difficulties in learning. It is probable that only a small number of children will require this system at any one time so it is reasonable to pool resources across several classes. It is not being suggested that most children will need this approach. Indeed, it is likely that the small curricular steps linked to specific materials and activities would be counter-productive and, for many, would slow down learning. Neither is it being suggested that children with learning difficulties should spend a disproportionate amount of time working through such a system. It will be important to add activities which help children to generalise and apply the skills practised. The effectiveness of this approach depends in part on how well it helps the teacher to monitor, and respond to, children's learning. This leads to issues about record-keeping which are the focus of the following chapter.

Chapter 9

Record-keeping

Why bother with keeping records about what children are learning or have learned? Teachers sometimes say that they can remember what they need to know about children's learning without spending time writing down detailed records. If that approach was ever sufficient, the ERA and specifically the NC have ensured that it is not enough now. The ex-student teacher who told me that he was not going to keep records of children's learning because he planned to become an inspector would find that the need for records, at any level, is increasing rather than diminishing!

Classroom records may be prospective (e.g. teaching plans for the long, medium or short term) or retrospective (e.g. children's learning, including developmental changes and curriculum-based assessment). Sometimes a short-term teaching plan can double as a record of a child's learning in specific activities. The focus of this chapter is on records of children's learning rather than on the writing of teaching plans. The latter has been discussed in chapters 3,4 and 5.

This chapter is in three parts: the first outlines records of children's learning in the context of the NC, the second discusses the purposes and types of records of individuals' learning which are maintained by the teacher (often in collaboration with care-givers) and the third part of the chapter reviews ways in which children might maintain their own records. Broader issues about record-keeping which are applicable to all children (e.g. the general form of reporting to care-givers) will not be explored in detail. The SEAC (1990a) materials on teacher assessment examine questions and possible practice concerning whole class and school record-keeping.

THE NATIONAL CURRICULUM AND RECORDS OF LEARNING

Nick Yapp, in *Bluff your Way in Teaching*, suggests that the purpose of record-keeping is: 'To make sure that teachers don't nip off at half past three every day' (Yapp 1987: 42). Record-keeping, he says, is a chance to fantasise and to write down what was supposed to happen, what the teacher wishes had happened, and what the teacher knows will never happen. Circular 8/90 (DES 1990f) sets out to curb such flippancy in relation to records of children's learning!

Research by Ted Wragg and his co-workers (1989) found that 55 per cent of teachers, in a sample of 901 primary teachers surveyed, anticipated that record-keeping, in relation to the NC, would be difficult (48 per cent) or very difficult (7 per cent). Work by Sarah Tann (1990) suggests that a concern about record-keeping continued once the NC had begun. She found, in a review of the first term of the NC in infant and first schools, that adequate monitoring and recording of children's learning was the teachers' chief concern. From evidence of HMI surveys, there is grounds for these concerns. Surveys to date have not commented specifically on record-keeping in relation to children with learning difficulties. HMI's first survey of the implementation of the NC (surveyed Summer 1989) noted that:

> The most common forms of record keeping ... did little to inform either future planning or provision in the core subjects.
> The great majority of schools fell short of what is required to fulfil the requirements of the National Curriculum, particularly in science. There is a need for greater clarity about the purposes served by records, for whom the recorded information is provided and the uses to be made of it.
>
> (HMI 1989a: paras 38, 42)

HMI's second report on the implementation of the NC (surveyed Autumn 1989) indicated that the NC was having a major impact on record-keeping: 'About four fifths of the schools were in the process of introducing new record-keeping policies or establishing revised arrangements' (HMI 1990d: para. 36). This endorses a comment by NCC (NCC 1989f) that teachers would need to 're-structure' record systems to bring them into line with the NC. However, HMI had doubts about the quality of this re-structuring:

Nearly a half of the new arrangements were, however, regarded as ineffective or inadequate. Most criticisms were directed at checklists, some of them very detailed, which provided only superficial information about the specific skills and levels of understanding and knowledge acquired by children.

(HMI 1990d: para. 37)

Despite these criticisms, HMI concluded that, overall, methods of record-keeping had improved since the previous term (i.e. the Summer 1989 survey). Positive developments included: greater standardisation of records; a wider range of areas recorded (both within and outside the core subjects); and the use of NC ATs, rather than place reached in published schemes, as the foci of records.

Given that teachers are concerned about record-keeping, why did HMI not find better practice? One answer must be the lack of time to think about the re-planning of record sheets in the light of the NC. It is easy to forget how rapidly the NC has come into being as the terms of the NC have been quickly adopted. I doubt if a commentator would now write (seriously), as happened in 1988, 'The teagat report...'.

Teachers and heads have received a succession of documents about the NC, from the consultation booklet on the NC (DES 1987) in July 1987 to rapid series of subject-specific working group reports, consultation reports, draft Orders, Orders, and, in some cases, revised Orders. Alongside these have been drafts and final versions of circulars and regulations as well as advisory documents from SEAC and NCC, and publications from professional, curricular and political groups. One reviewer estimated that it took nine and a half hours to read only the SEAC (1990a) materials on classroom assessment!

Debate has shifted rapidly from principles to practicalities. Teachers, especially those working with children at key stage 1, have had very little time to read and review the basic curriculum documents, let alone to devise useful and relevant record sheets. Even if this was done (as, for example, in some authorities, by setting up teams of 'super-teachers' to produce blueprint plans and record sheets), the slow arrival of cross-curricular documents has been frustrating. It is interesting to consider how the NC would have been received and implemented in primary and special schools if the cross-curricular documents had come out before, rather than after, the core and some other foundation subject documents. Schools which were quick off the mark in re-drafting record sheets may, because of the sequence of publication of NC materials, be left with a legacy of a strong bias towards the core subjects. This may, in turn, be further reinforced by the pattern of SATs which are skewed towards the core subjects only.

We need to think imaginatively about how time can be created for essential non-teaching but teaching-related activities. Some LEAs have allocated 'assessment support teachers' to give class teachers time for observation, assessment and record-keeping for, say, half a day each week. Whether these arrangements will continue under the new funding arrangements is still to be seen. An enlightened governing body might make such an appointment (perhaps shared among several schools). Greater use of collaborative teaching, in which two (or more) teachers work jointly with their classes, might encourage more flexibility of teaching group size and so give time for one teacher to carry out assessments and record-keeping. The use of various adults in the classroom (discussed in chapter 8) might also mean that some kinds of record-keeping could be done by an adult other than the class teacher. There is also room for using audio and video records as well as or instead of the more usual written accounts. A good video of, say, a class drama or science project can convey more vividly than can a written account the breadth and depth of learning taking place.

Some schools have 'star child' meetings in which all staff meet to discuss individual children's learning. Usually staff will meet for a short while (perhaps just 15 minutes) on one or two mornings per week, before school starts, specifically for 'star child' sessions. Teachers take it in turn to review the learning of several children in their classes so that all staff can share relevant information, offer suggestions and keep up to date with individual children's progress. If all staff are involved, including ancillary and support staff, then a broad picture of the child can be shared. Inevitably the children who feature in star child sessions tend to be children who stand out in some way, perhaps because they are causing concern or are the focus of a statement of SEN (or, in the future, perhaps, of temporary exceptions for disapplication or modification of the NC). The star child discussions run a risk of reinforcing prejudices unless they are chaired skilfully; the discussion leader needs to ensure that assertions and reports are supported with evidence and that the discussion focuses on the positive and the relevant. Given these provisos, star child sessions are potentially an excellent way of drawing together information from a range of people who have worked with the same child at different times and in various situations. Usually such sessions are not formally minuted and so are not a part of formal, written records.

Greater use could also be made of diary records between home and school to which parents, teachers and children all contribute. These can form a natural record of children's learning and development and are especially useful for children who say relatively little to parents/teachers about what they have done at home/school. Shiela Wolfendale (1989; see also RDAMP 1989, appendix 1) has worked extensively on ways to amalgamate home and school-based information about children's learning. The *All About Me* profile is one approach which, like the diaries mentioned above, can be used for children starting formal schooling but has applications across the primary age range. Some schools for children with severe learning difficulties also use diary records to convey home–school information. Without these records, there would be little information between home and school about the children's daily activities. This lack of communication arises from the children's poor memory or linguistic skills as well as the possible distance betweeen home and special school which means that the children are taken to the school by special bus or taxi, unaccompanied by parents/care-givers. If successive diaries are saved by the school, with other records, a broad account of the child's attainments and experiences may be stored.

Records and accountability

The emphasis in the ERA (and the NC specifically) on teachers' accountability is likely to lead to an increased emphasis on the importance of record-keeping. Teachers' records of their teaching and children's past and projected learning will provide the data which, combined with evidence of what children have learned, will show whether or not the school has kept to its legal obligation to teach the NC. As a result, schools will also need to find ways of storing, effectively and efficiently, the bulky records of children's learning.

The statutory position is that, through regulations passed in 1989 (no. 1261), each governing body of a maintained school must keep a curricular record for each child registered at the school. Schools are also required by law to report annually, as a minimum, to parents about their children's attainments in all NC subjects and 'other activities'. This applies as soon as children commence NC POSs (i.e. from age 5 for most children). Circular 8/90 (DES 1990f) details the expected content of annual reports to parents. Reports at ages 5, 6, 8, 9 and 10 (i.e. non-reporting ages at key stages 1 and 2) can be in subjects, profile components and/or ATs. At the reporting ages (i.e. ages 7 and 11 for most children at key stages 1 and 2), the reports to parents must show NC levels attained for each profile component and subject (not necessarily individual SOAs) for the foundation subjects for which Orders have been made. Parents have a right to request, and be given, information about their children's levels on individual ATs at the end of the key stages. Obviously this reporting will be eased if the teacher's formal records dovetail with the annual report forms. Some schools are using micro-computer programs to store and transfer some of this type of data. The notes kept by a teacher purely for his or her use are not a formal part of the child's curriculum record and so do not have to be disclosed.

These regulations apply to all children but there is an even stronger force for keeping detailed records for children who have difficulties in learning, particularly if these are allied to a statement of SEN under the 1981 Education Act. Interestingly, Carolyn Blyth and Fiona Wallace (1988) found, in their study of record-keeping, that reception class teachers considered it necessary for nurseries to maintain and to pass on records concerning only children with SEN. The reception class teachers preferred not to be 'prejudiced' by receiving records on other children. Some teachers might disagree with the latter point but the findings do illustrate an implicit recognition by teachers of the particular importance of monitoring and recording the learning and development of children with SEN.

Children with learning difficulties may, in order to demonstrate progress, require much more detailed records than are needed for other children. Formal annual reports to care-givers must include indications of any aspects of the NC which have been disapplied. If large parts of the NC have been disapplied then it is up to the school to decide what information to pass on to the care-givers. Circular 8/90 states that:

It must be a matter of good practice for schools to amplify with narrative commentary ... the reports on all pupils with learning difficulties which lead either to exemptions (whether on individual or multiple ATs) or to slow progress from one level to the next.

(DES 1990f: para. 21)

It would be logical and sensible to link closely these records with annual reviews for children who have statements of SEN. The statement should, by law, be reviewed annually and the teachers' records will be important in showing whether learning targets have been met and how, if at all, the statement should be amended. However, research into the working of the 1981 Education Act (RDAMP 1989) found that statements tended to be written vaguely and so mask discrepancies between a child's needs and the available provision. Similarly, HMI's review of children with statements in ordinary schools found that statements were of 'mediocre quality ... lacked detail, gave little guidance on the pupil's curricular needs and were inadequate for the planning of an educational programme' (HMI 1990c: para. 45). Thus, one of the benefits of the NC may be in sharpening considerably the wording and foci of statements although, for many children, targets will be wider than the NC (e.g. including social and self-help skills).

No specific record sheet is included in Circular 8/90 but the approach behind Records of Achievement is praised as crystallising much good practice. The rest of this chapter considers possible formats and functions of record sheets linked to the NC for children showing difficulties in learning.

RECORDS OF LEARNING/TEACHING MAINTAINED BY THE TEACHER

One of the main purposes behind record-keeping in schools is to maintain continuity and progression in children's learning. The centrality of these themes in the NC means that record-keeping has become a central issue in discussions about implementing the NC. Records of learning for children with learning difficulties may aim to fulfil some additional and very specific purposes. These include: monitoring learning in relation to particular learning targets, monitoring stages of learning, noting various factors which impede or promote learning (such as membership of specific work groups and the effectiveness of different teaching methods) and checking that the child experiences a broad curriculum on a daily and weekly basis.

The types of record which might meet each of these purposes will be discussed and possible outlines given for appropriate records. These outlines are given tentatively as possible starting points, not blueprints. Individual teachers will know what would fit their own ways of working. The need for teachers to devise record systems which suit, perhaps uniquely, their own schools, has been emphasised by Tom Christie (a member of the Manchester-based STAIR consortium which developed one approach to SATs). He stated: 'I firmly believe that ultimately we need 25,000 recording systems. I believe it because I think that we need 25,000 different school environments' (Christie 1990).

Monitoring learning in relation to specific learning targets

Records of learning in specific curriculum-based activities are likely to be a useful adjunct to broader and class records which include children with difficulties in learning. A division of target activities into smaller steps (see chapter 5) links naturally with a record sheet showing these steps and the child's progress through them. Such records need to show:

*   Possible sequence of steps for a particular learning target (bearing in mind that these are guidelines and that the child may jump around the steps, especially in activities, such as creative writing, which cannot be classified into a single hierarchical sequence),
*   When the child started activities towards the target,
*   Teaching/learning approaches used,
*   Other information about the context and circumstances in which the learning took place,
*   NC ATs to which the steps link,
*   Date on which the child was first able to complete the target,
*   Series of dates on which this achievement was checked,
*   Any links with the child's statement.

Some advantages of these records are that they:

- Focus on what the child can do,
- Have clear implications for teaching.
- Build up into a detailed record of part(s) of that child's learning, showing continuity and progression,
- Can be maintained by the teacher and child together,
- Give the child frequent feedback about his or her progress,
- Are individualised, so that one child is not being compared directly with other children,
- Can be easily understood by care-givers and other adults (important if several adults work with the child; see chapter 8),
- Can show patterns over time (e.g. that a child needs regular fortnightly revision of sight vocabulary words),
- Can be used as evidence if they relate to a child's statement.

Figure 9.1 is a sample record sheet which contains all of the features summarised, although this is at the expense of having much room to write. If classroom records are to be useful, they need, like Ordnance Survey maps or horse racing form books, to combine succinctness with good quality, relevant information and to be uncluttered by the irrelevant! No doubt, over the next few years, many schemes will be devised, tried and modified before we arrive at some commonly accepted and used conventions. The NCC (NCC 1990b) has already stated that DES, HMI and SEAC have agreed to adopt common conventions for subject areas, attainment targets, statements of attainments and levels within these (e.g. En 3/2b).

This degree of detail will be needed for relatively few children and for only some activities in most mainstream primary classes. It would be unrealistic and inappropriate to try to maintain records containing this much detail for all children in the class. However, if some records do contain this level of detail, they can double as both teaching plans and learning records. This approach was used in one school in which I worked. The children kept these records in their work folders (for core subjects only) and would work with the teacher to fill them in when an activity had been finished. These children, who were some way behind their classmates, seemed to obtain a sense of achievement as the columns were filled in. The small steps listed meant that most children moved

Figure 9.1 Sample record sheet for an individual child having difficulties
          in a specific curricular area
(Key: O = begun; Ø = achieved; ● = checked)

NAME: Sammy	CLASS: Year 3	
POS: English, KS 1 ACTIVITY: Story → ATs 1/1b,1/2c,1/3a;2/1d,2/2d,2/3c		
Programme of study	*Assessment*	
Activities	*Evidence of learning*	*Dates*
Listen to story tapes and discuss with adult	Recounted one incident	O 10 Sept Ø 14 Sept ● 1 Oct
Listen to story tapes and discuss alternative endings	Drew imagined next event	O 24 Sept Ø 19 Nov ●
Invent stories using picture sequences	Told story from 3-picture sequence on to tape	O 24 Sept Ø 3 Dec ●
Invent story from initial stimulus		O Ø ●
Observation notes and action: Sammy enjoys puppets. Develop ways of using these to stimulate story telling. Sammy's parents keen to help Sammy at home with developing stories. Lend Sammy's parents story tapes from toy library to use at home. Discuss learning aims for Sammy with them, e.g. encourage Sammy's evaluation of stories.		

quickly through them. More global targets would have taken these
children many months or terms to move from one target to the
next.

The least useful type of record is probably the series of SOAs to
be listed for all children in the class and against which every child
will eventually be ticked off. There must surely be a strong
temptation to ignore for several months such an arid record and
then to go through the whole class at some crucial date, such as
before a parents' meeting, and quickly enter, perhaps undated,

ticks and crosses for every child. The only use for this type of
summary sheet is as an administrative record rather than as a guide
for teaching; it cannot include the necessary detail about how, as
well as what, children are learning. Detailed records such as those
described earlier could provide information for a summary sheet.

Monitoring stages of learning

For some children, difficulties may arise because they learn things
initially but then fail to retain the skills or processes and/or cannot
use them in new contexts. For these children it is useful to have
record sheets which, again tied to specific activities, record various
stages of learning (see chapter 3). Figure 9.2 gives an example of
a record sheet to record stages of learning.

Noting various factors which foster or impede learning

There is a strong temptation, when discussing records, to make the
areas which warrant recording more and more numerous. All
records are inadequate in that there is always more which could be
said or written about individuals' learning. However, including
comment about school-based factors which foster or impede
learning is useful (see chapter 4 for a discussion of some relevant
factors) but is only worthwhile if the information is used. Some
writers refer to children with difficulties in learning as 'the hard to
reach' or 'hard to teach' which, rightly, puts the onus on the
teacher rather than the child.

Most teachers can think of children who, while making
relatively slow progress in some curricular areas, do very well in
others or in particular contexts. The process of writing down
details about the contexts in which the child is successful helps to
focus attention on these and therefore on how they might be
maximised. A brief way of doing this would be to have a summary
sheet of notes with the child's profile which contains helpful and
limiting aspects of the classroom situation for that particular child,
including specific and detailed evidence for the statement.
Discussion with the child and his or her care-givers about more
and less successful teaching methods helps to fill in the picture
and to show whether suspected preferences or dislikes are
confirmed by the child.

Figure 9.2 Sample record sheet to show stages of learning for an individual child in relation to a specific curricular area
(Key: O = begun; Ø = achieved; ● = checked)

NAME: Tracy A.		CLASS: Year 3	
POS: Maths, KS 2		ACTIVITY: Adition to 10 →AT 3/2a	

Programme of study		*Assessment*	
Learning stages	*Activities*	*Evidence of learning*	*Dates*
Acquisition	Add to 10, with teacher, using Unifix	Built tower of bricks, counted correct total (up to 12)	O 15 Jan Ø 11 Feb ● 1 Mar ● 8 Apr
Fluency	Snap and other quick number games	Orally, added domino cards correctly (10 in one minute)	O 7 Feb Ø 10 Mar ● 8 Apr
Generalisation	Shopping games in class 'market'	Added money correctly, using coins, totalling up to 10p	O 4 Feb Ø 9 Mar ● 8 Apr
Adaptation/ application	Applying add facts in map drawing	Drew map of classroom, talked about equal sides 'made up' differently	O 22 Apr Ø 25 Apr ●

Diary type records built up over time may also show significant patterns of behaviour which are lost in the more fine-grained records of curriculum-based assessment. If a child has a folder containing examples of his or her work from pre-infant school days onwards, then diary type records can be added to the folder. This folder becomes a continuing record of a child's achievements and should include the child's evaluative comments about his or her work. Children with learning difficulties may have attended pre-infant school assessment units and, if so, information and possibly children's work from there can be included in this folder.

Checking that the child has a broad curriculum on a daily, weekly or termly basis

There is a variety of record sheets available for the NC. These range from photocopied sheets developed by staff in a particular school to glossy, commercially produced planning and summary grids. On the one hand, home-made record sheets are more likely to fit the purpose and to be used, but there is a risk of teachers spending time re-inventing the wheel; on the other hand, commercial schemes may appear to be definitive and foolproof, to save much agonising and tedious listing of ATs and so forth but they may be extremely boring and in the end may not be used very effectively.

The experiences from the trialling of SATs and their accompanying record sheets show that teachers disliked the proformas provided and revised these. This might have been a reflection of the record sheets but it also illustrates the strong tradition of primary teachers constructing their own materials. Even LEA-derived NC record sheets, devised by teachers in the authority, are reportedly changed by other teachers using them in school. This seems to me to be a constructive strategy which helps teachers to have ownership of the materials and therefore to make better use of them. However, such individualism is at odds with pressures to use the NC to create greater uniformity across schools.

Most of the commercial and home-made record-keeping schemes which I have seen have focused on individual subjects, perhaps bringing together the three core areas in a summary sheet. Children with difficulties in learning have tended to do many activities in 'basic skills' at the expense of the broader curriculum (see chapters 2 and 3) and record systems which emphasise the NC core may reinforce this pattern.

The appropriate record sheet for recording an overview of, say, weekly learning will reflect the orientation taken by the school towards planning the whole curriculum. For some schools a weekly check sheet might contain HMI's areas of learning and experience (DES 1985) while for other schools a simple listing of NC subjects, RE and cross-curricular themes can be a useful antidote to curricular narrowing. This type of check could be used for all children but would be particularly important for children who, for example, repeatedly carried out additional English activities and for whom the teacher suspected that other areas were being neglected. The overview could be completed by the teacher (perhaps using two different symbols for work planned and for work actually carried out). This would show where a child avoided or favoured activities (e.g. tending to carry out technology work in preference to written language, where both were possible activities, such as in the development of a cross-curricular topic). The teacher could choose to focus on two or three children each week when completing this type of record. Over a term all children would then have been recorded for one week and the children on whom there was a need to focus more strongly (perhaps because they were often absent) would have been monitored for two weeks. The record sheet could be completed through teachers' recalling activities done by children and/or by using children to make the record. The following section explores ways in which children can maintain records of learning goals and attainments.

RECORDS MAINTAINED BY THE CHILD

There are many ways in which children can maintain records of their learning goals and attainments. To do this ought to help both the child and the teacher. This section reviews four broad types of child-maintained records: records of the learning process (including goal setting and attainments) in one activity, evaluative records of learning, daily or weekly records of activities carried out, and summative records of learning targets.

Child-maintained records are important because of the links with developing children's autonomy in learning and promoting self-confidence. Both of these are things which children who have had difficulties in mastering school tasks may lack and which therefore further impede learning. A vicious circle is created in which the child 'fails', loses confidence, becomes more dependent on the teacher, loses autonomy and so is back to greater dependence on the teacher. Turning this into a virtuous circle, in which success in learning leads to increased confidence and motivation and so to further learning, is one of the skills of teaching.

Child-maintained records in specific tasks

Some activities lend themselves to a record built up by the child which shows the process that he or she is going through in reaching a particular goal. For example, a story can be recorded in a zig-zag book containing successive versions (see figure 9.3).

This helps children to see how their work is developing. A similar approach can be used for successive plans in making a technological model. Children who perceive themselves as being of low ability seem to be particularly helped by seeing that an early, rough piece of work is part of the process towards a more polished, final version. Similarly, they see that all children go from rougher, early versions to more polished, later versions. Successive writers' drafts illustrate the same point (although the use of word processors may mean that this evidence is no longer being produced). One well-known children's writer sent extracts from successive drafts of one of his stories to a class whom I taught. The children (all of whom had learning and/or behavioural difficulties) were astonished that a published author did not write the final story at his first attempt. They were surprised that, just like their first drafts, the author's early attempts at a story were messy and incomplete. This experience seemed to help them to accept that they also would make better stories by trying to improve first drafts.

Child-maintained evaluative records of learning

Children's evaluation of their own work can be linked to records. Peter Gurney (1990) has reviewed a range of research which investigated links between children's self-esteem and school achievements. He observes:

> Arrange for a failing child to achieve success in a task and what is he likely to say? 'It was a fluke,' or 'I was lucky.' The evidence of success is likely to be rejected because it is discrepant with his self-concept.

(Gurney 1990: 9)

Peter Gurney argues that it is important for teachers to help such children to shift to accepting that they themselves have control over the type of result that they obtain. A discussion with an adult about what is good about the work and how it could be improved helps to keep children's evaluations both recognised and realistic.

A Coventry primary head, Julie Barsby (1991), has devised a series of ways in which children can evaluate their work. She was particularly interested in developing children's evaluation of their

Figure 9.3 A record of developing a piece of writing (by Simon, age 8)
(a) Planning the writing using a *Breakthrough* folder (at a later stage, making a handwritten plan)
(b) Writing the first draft
(c) Typing the draft into a word processor (at a later stage, making improvements to successive versions)

(a)

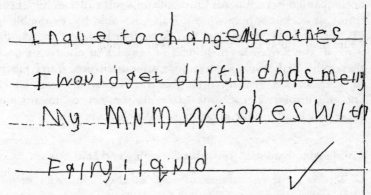

(b)

I have to change my clothes
I would get dirty and smelly
My Mum washes with
Fairy liquid ✓

(c)

```
I have   to  change   my   clothes.

I would get  dirty  and   smelly.

My Mum  washes   with Fairy liquid.
```

creative writing. To encourage this, she invented various gauges which were placed around the classroom. These home-made gauges included a device like a large toothpaste tube from which a roll of coloured cloth could be unrolled, an elephant with a retractable trunk, and a sequence of smiley faces. Each child, having completed some writing, would then go, with a friend, to one of these gauges, and discuss how the piece of writing was to be rated. Various criteria were discussed with the children beforehand and included: how interesting was the story, was it easy to follow, and could it have been made more exciting? The children discussed how far to move the indicator in order to give a rating on specific criteria for the piece of work. When Julie Barsby assessed systematically whether or not these gauges helped children to become more self-evaluative she found that their use was associated with more frequent and more appropriate evaluations.

Some schools encourage children to make evaluative comments about all of their work. When written work is completed, it is accompanied by comments from both an adult and the child. Even if not all work is annotated in this way, it would be reasonable to do this for work which goes into a current folder of the child's work. If the school keeps folders of samples of children's work then individual children can choose, after discussion, which pieces of work should go into their folders. Similarly, classroom or corridor displays can include spaces for viewers' comments and these may be about the presentation as well as content.

Child-maintained daily records of learning and activities

Children can be encouraged to maintain their own daily records of activities planned and carried out. Although this applies to all children, it is particularly important for children with difficulties or disillusionment about school tasks because child-maintained records emphasise the child's active part in monitoring learning activities. One strategy involves children posting tickets when they have started or finished particular activities. For example, the teacher might set out various activities which are accompanied by pieces of card (colour coded for the activity: e.g. blue for maths, yellow for reading, red for science). When the children have finished the activity, they write their names on the cards and post the tickets into a box or tray. The teacher then has a record, provided by the children, of who has been engaged in which activities over the session or the day. Another strategy entails children writing, on an overall plan, the activities in which they have been engaged. Some teachers begin the day by going through, with a whole class or group, the activities which individuals will be doing. These are written on to a sheet of paper, whiteboard or OHP transparency to form a timetable for the day (or week). As children complete their sections, they tick off their names.

Child-maintained longer term summative records

Children can keep continuing summative records of their learning. Some curricular areas lend themselves to a record sheet which shows successive steps towards various goals. An obvious example is a record sheet showing aspects of learning spelling or decoding parts of words. Figure 9.4 shows an example of a 'phonics' record sheet in which the teacher started by assessing the sounds which the child could decode. (The sequence of 'sounds' was taken from the *Classroom Index of Phonic Resources* [Herbert and Davies-Jones 1984]; see chapter 8.) Squares representing these known sounds were then coloured in by the child. As the child learned further sounds, these were also coloured in (and dated). Different colours were used for different terms in the school year so that the chart also showed some idea of the rate at which new sounds were being learned. The record was readily understood by the children and, as it was linked explicitly with the classroom resources, children could also tell from the chart which set of work they should go on to next.

It has become popular to encourage children to monitor their own learning but at times this seems to be done in a way which lacks much purpose or coherence. In one school, I saw children colouring in windows on a stylised drawing of a house (drawn and photocopied by the teacher on to individual sheets) to show how many stories they had written that week. As this had no qualitative aspect and was subsequently thrown away it seemed to have no value to either the children or the teacher.

Lesley Webb, writing in 1967, rated record-keeping to be as important as the teacher's personal attitudes in identifying children in need of extra help. While that function of record-keeping remains today, it is also vital in the new climate of accountability.

Figure 9.4 Example of a phonics record sheet on which children recorded their successive attainments

PHONIC RECORD SHEET:

1	2	3	4	5	6	7	8	9	10	11	12	13	14	15	16	17	18	19	20
vis. disc.	aud disc.	cons	a	e	i	o	u	short vowel revision	b/d	ee	$\overline{oo}$	oo	ll ss ff	nt st ck	sh	ch	th	wh	ph

21	22	23	24	25	26	27	28	29	30	31	32	33	34	35	36	37	38	39	40
shr sch thr tch	pl fl cl	pr cr fr	sw sn sm	dw tw qu	scr spr squ spl	a-e	i-e	o-e	u-e	magic e revision	ai	ar	au	aw	ay	ēā	ea	er	ew

41	42	43	44	45	46	47	48	49	50	51	52	53	54	55	56	57	58
ie ei	ir	oa	oe ie ue	oi	or	ou	$\overline{ow}$	ow	oy	ur	y	pref.	suff.	kn mb ght wr	soft c+ g	-r	ms

Name:
Date started:

Source: Herbert and Davies-Jones (1984)

Chapter 10

SATs and children with learning difficulties

> It is not possible to describe a standard of attainment that should be reached by all or most children [by the end of primary school].
>
> (CACE 1967: para. 551)

This statement from the Plowden Report of 1967 stands in stark contrast to the orientation of the NC. The NC embodies continuous teacher assessments of children's learning, regarded generally as difficult but desirable and uncontroversial, and summative assessments at the ends of key stages. The purpose of the summative assessments, and conceptual difficulties in combining formative with summative assessments have been widely debated (e.g. Flude and Hammer 1990, Nuttall 1988, 1989).

SUMMATIVE ASSESSMENT IN THE NATIONAL CURRICULUM

Summative assessment at the ends of keys stages comprises teacher assessments, standard assessment tasks (SATs) and non-statutory assessment tasks. It is the SATs element which has been most contentious. The foci of SATs have progressively narrowed since the recommendations of the TGAT Report (DES/WO 1988a). The TGAT Report suggested that, at the end of key stage 2, three or four SATs might be given. These might focus on mathematical/ scientific understanding, literacy and humanities, and aesthetics. This has been narrowed to the core subjects only. There will be no statutory requirement to administer SATs in technology, history and geography at the end of key stage 1 or, probably, at the end of key stage 2. Instead, these subjects are to be assessed through non-statutory assessment tasks. These will be less time-consuming and narrower in focus than SATs but still nationally prescribed. It is not clear how the other foundation subjects will be assessed at the ends of the key stages.

SATs within the core subjects have also become more narrowly focused than was originally envisaged. SATs at the end of key stage 1 will focus on a sample, rather than all, of the core ATs. At key stage 1 there will be one SAT (comprising several activities) to assess nine ATs, plus a separate reading assessment based on miscue analysis. Seven of the ATs will be assessed by all teachers of children in the age group and the other two ATs will be chosen by teachers from four of the maths and three of the science targets. The SAT at key stage 1 will not be cross-curricular, as recommended in the TGAT Report, but will consist of a series of subject-specific activities each dealing with one or two ATs.

The combining of some ATs which will be assessed for all children (except for children for whom assessment arrangements have been disapplied) along with a limited choice of other ATs means that the SATs testing can meet several different purposes. If the SATs have good validity and reliability, then the results of SATs could be used to compare children, schools, classes, teachers or LEAs on the common ATs. Other SAT assessments of maths and science, although not applied to all children, will enable the monitoring of parts of the NC to be carried out.

The successive narrowing of SATs can be interpreted in various ways. At one level, it is an endorsement of the importance of continuous teacher assessment. Overall assessment at the ends of the key stages has not been reduced; it is the balance between SATs and teacher assessment which has changed, away from standard, nationally prescribed tasks. Circular 8/90 on records of achievement (DES 1990f) stated that parents who request details by NC level of their child's attainments at the ends of key stages should be given this information for all relevant ATs, not just those assessed through SATs.

However, it has been argued that the narrowing focus of SATs reflects the higher status of curricular areas to remain within SATs; the 'important' curricular areas are assessed through SATs while 'less important' areas are left to the more fuzzy, continuous teacher assessments. The exclusion of speaking and listening from the key stage 1 SAT may be seen as diminishing the importance of oral work and encouraging teachers to give less time to developing these skills. A more pragmatic response is that the piloting of SATs showed that, given existing staffing levels, it would be impossible to make SATs as broad as originally envisaged in the TGAT Report. On various grounds (e.g. time, and distortion of the curriculum), any narrowing of SATs could be interpreted as educationally beneficial. It means that SATs may be less intrusive, may take up less time at the ends of the key stages and so free teachers to get on with teaching and evaluating the broader curriculum. Another, perhaps cynical, response to the narrowing of SATs is to say that this reflects diminishing government confidence in the NC. If the assessment process is thorough, wide ranging, reliable and valid *and* it turns out that, over time, the NC does not seem to be raising standards, then the government has to defend this. This leads to consideration of SATs for children who have difficulties in school-based learning. There are several general issues about SATs which have specific implications for these children.

NC levels as end-points or stages

The first issue concerns whether the levels on ATs are end-points or broad stages. This can be described as conceptualising the levels as either mile markers (see figure 10.1(a)) or pathways between the mile markers (see figure 10.1(b)). For example, if a child is described as being 'at level 2', does this mean that he or she has mastered the SOAs at that level or that he or she is working towards level 2? This issue was referred to in chapter 5 in connection with planning learning. It is perhaps more critical in the current context, as it dictates the level at which the child is reported to be.

The NC documents, in general, adhere to the levels on ATs as 'mile markers'. This is clear in SEAC's advice on NC assessment arrangements:

> There are no intermediate points on the scale. A pupil is assessed as achieving a particular level – 2, say – when the relevant criteria are satisfied. Up to that time, the pupil is reported as having achieved level 1 and to be working towards level 2.
>
> (SEAC 1989: para. 6)

Thus, according to SEAC, the criteria for the levels on ATs are minima, so that a child who is between levels would be described as being at the lower level. For example, a child who can give a

Figure 10.1 Levels on attainment targets
(a) NC levels as 'mile markers'
(b) NC levels as pathways
(c) level 1 as a pathway and other levels as mile markers

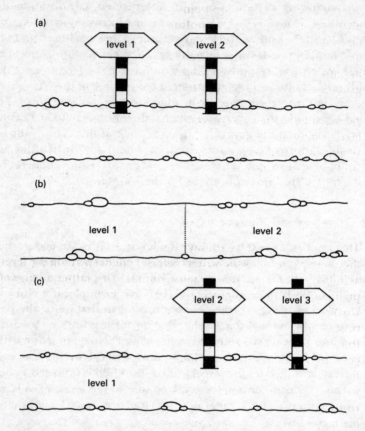

sensible estimate of the number of objects in a group of ten (Ma 4/1), and who is moving towards being able to give a sensible estimate when shown a group of twenty objects (Ma 4/2), is at level 1 even if the teacher regards the child as 'nearly' at level 2. This is reasonable if one is striving for greater precision and specificity in assessment statements. It differs from the way in which teachers tend to describe children's attainments, which is more in line with levels as broad stages. For example, teachers often refer to a child being at or on book 3 of a reading scheme when the child is working towards being able to read book 3.

The mile marker approach means that there is no level to describe children who have not yet reached the criteria for level 1. If level 1 represents an end-point (mile marker), then children with learning difficulties may be designated as being at a 'level 0' or 'pre-level 1'. The same point may apply to many children on entry to compulsory schooling and has repercussions for describing levels on NC 'baseline assessments'. To describe children who do not meet level 1 criteria as being at 'level 0' implies that those children have no educational attainments in the given area. This is obviously misleading, given the vast range of skills and understanding which children may have, although not yet reaching the level 1 criteria. The Cox Report (DES/WO 1989c) takes a mile marker approach to levels, treating them as minima (e.g. para 15.32) except in the case of level 1:

> We understand that level 1 is intended to encompass a wide range of attainment, from those pupils who have barely begun to learn, to those who are very close to level 2.
>
> (DES/WO 1989c: para. 12.5)

This implies a broad (pathway) view of level 1, although, later in the same paragraph, the writers refer to children attaining level 1 as if, like other levels, it represents minima. This rather ambiguous position is illustrated diagrammatically in figure 10.1(c). Uncertainty about whether level 1 is a point or a broad phase is reflected in the variety of terms, such as 'within level 1', 'working towards level 1' and 'approaching level 1', which is used by commentators to refer to children 'below' level 1 but still within the NC. This does not seem to happen in relation to later levels, as writers accept the levels as representing minima there. One repercussion of this fudging about level 1 concerns potential inconsistencies when following the rules to combine AT levels into profile components and subjects.

Differentiation by task or by outcome

The three development agencies involved in piloting SATs (CATS, NFER and STAIR) took different approaches. One difference between them was in whether they chose to differentiate children's attainments by tasks or by outcome. In the former, children are designated as being at a particular level and given appropriate tasks for their level. This is crudely similar to dividing children in a class into ability groups and allocating work accordingly (red group do practical work, cutting up apples and labelling the parts; blue group do fractions workcards; green group do problems which involve using fractions, etc.). Differentiation by outcome is illustrated by the activities which teachers often do with a new class, such as asking all of the children to swim from one side of a swimming pool to the other. As a result of watching all of the children do this same exercise, the teacher sub-divides the class into 'non-swimmers', 'beginners', 'proficient swimmers', etc.

There are strengths and weaknesses in both approaches. For children who find school-based learning difficult, differentiation by task may be more encouraging. They are not faced with tasks outside their capabilities. However, this means that the children may be the victims of inappropriate teacher expectations; if the teacher does not anticipate that the child will succeed on a task then the child will not get the chance to try it. This is less likely to happen if there have been good, continuous assessments of children's learning, although these would not prevent low expectations of a child. The Standard Tests and Assessment Implementation Research (STAIR) Consortium argued for differentiation by task in SATs on the basis that the teacher's continuous assessment will alert her or him to the appropriate task for individual children. Thus, this makes the SAT assessment build on the preceding teacher assessments.

The TGAT Report (DES/WO 1988a) recommended differentiation by outcome at key stage 1 and differentiation by task, if necessary, at later key stages. Differentiation by outcome means that children who find learning difficult are not judged initially as being incapable of some tasks. All children have the same chance to show what they can do. Many tasks could be curtailed when a child begins to have difficulties. However, to be faced repeatedly with tasks which are too difficult is very demoralising and so differentiation by outcome requires very sensitive handling by teachers. This applies both before and after the tasks, as it makes it easier for children to compare attainments and for classmates who have been unable to complete tasks to feel 'shown up'. The NFER and CATS consortia have based their developments of SATs on differentiation by outcome.

In practice, SATs could combine differentiation by outcome and differentiation by task. This could be done within an activity, whereby children might all have the same starting point but might then branch off into different tasks depending on attainments on the first activity. For example, children might sort 2D and 3D shapes into sets (Ma 10/1a). For children who made only two sets (2D and 3D), the follow-up task might be to draw the shapes and describe them (Ma 10/1b). For children who sorted the shapes by geometric shape as well as by number of dimensions, the follow-up activity might be to describe each type of shape (Ma 10/2a). When given the shapes to sort initially, some children might spontaneously talk about various different ways of sorting the shapes (Ma 10/3). SATs could also combine differentiation by outcome and by task by varying these across activities. For example, children could be given the same writing activity (differentiation by outcome) but a series of spoken language activities which vary according to individual children's expected attainments (differentiation by task).

The key stage 1 SAT will use mainly differentiation by task (Hofkins 1990) so that, for most activities, if the teacher believes a child to be capable of level 3, assessment will focus on this. If the child can do level 3, then levels 1 and 2 will be assumed. This will reduce time spent carrying out SATs but presumes that there is clear continuity between successive levels. Queries about this were discussed in chapter 5.

Age as the focus for timing of SATs

The TGAT Report (DES/WO 1988a) advocated that age should be the basic criterion for deciding when a child should complete SATs (and other summative assessments). In other words, all 7-year olds and all 11-year olds (unless exempted through the statement of SEN or direction for temporary exceptions) should be carrying out SATs regardless of either where they are likely to come on the ten identified levels within each subject or how they are grouped for teaching. This has been modified in later documents to provide more flexibility, so that children might do SATs with their teaching group rather than according to chronological ages. In general, SATs will be carried out when the majority of children in the teaching group are at the reporting ages (i.e. ages 7 and 11 in primary schools). This would suggest that a 9-year old in a teaching group with 7-year olds for, say, English, might do English SATs at the same time as those children.

Assessments of individuals within groups

There are many issues to be sorted out concerning valid and reliable assessments of individual children working in collaborative groups. The issues are not specific to children with difficulties in learning. Children who lack confidence, children who are perceived as low-attaining by classmates and children who find group situations difficult to handle are all likely to do less well in group contexts than they would if working independently. Resources may also be a critical factor. For example, an activity to assess children's understanding of magnetism could produce different apparent attainments depending on whether every child in the group has access to a set of materials or whether limited resources are shared among the group.

Individuals to carry out the assessments

The Order on assessment at key stage 1 states that teacher assessment should be carried out by 'a teacher' but it does not specify who should carry out the SAT assessment. Circular 8/90 (DES 1990f) states that at key stage 1 most teacher assessments and SATs will be carried out by the class teacher. In practice, an SEN support teacher might work through SATs with individuals or small groups of children, taking care that, for example, the language of the instructions has been understood. The support teacher might arrange for computer keyboards (including Concept keyboards), rather than pencil and paper, to be used as a means of recording.

SEAC (1990b) has advised that, if children usually have support staff help, that support should be there also when those children are involved in SATs. Presumably this might mean that, for example, a speech therapist rather than the class teacher might carry out the SAT. This is an important aspect of helping children to show what they are able to do. However, if the school has single age group classes for children at the reporting ages, it may have the effect of concentrating support staff in a few classes while SATs and teacher assessments are being carried out.

Aggregation of assessments

The Order for key stage 1 assessment and accompanying Circular 9/90 (DES 1990g) give precise rules for aggregation of assessments and how to deal with 'gaps' in AT attainments. The following examples illustrate how assessment for children with various difficulties in learning might be aggregated. These are all relatively straightforward examples, but there are potential anomalies in aggregating results (University of Warwick 1990).

Assessment for Brent

Brent has good oral language skills but finds written language tasks (reading, writing and spelling) difficult.

PC1 AT1 Speaking and listening   – level 3
PC2 AT2 Reading   – level 1
PC3 AT3 Writing   – level 1 (weighted 7)
PC3 AT4 Spelling   – level 1 (weighted 2)
PC3 AT5 Handwriting   – level 1 (weighted 1)
                        so PC3 =   level 1

Reported Assessment for English: level 2.

Assessment for Mandy

Mandy finds all of the core subjects difficult and is making slow progress in most curricular areas.

PC1 AT1 Speaking and listening   – level 1
PC2 AT2 Reading   – level 1
PC3 AT3 Writing   – level 1 (weighted 7)
PC3 AT4 Spelling   – level 1 (weighted 2)
PC3 AT5 Handwriting   – level 1 (weighted 1)
                        so PC3 =   level 1

Reported Assessment for English: level 1.

Assessment for Chris

Chris has hearing impairments but can carry out many aspects of the English ATs through alternative communication systems.

PC1 AT1 Speaking and listening   – level 2 (with sign)
PC2 AT2 Reading   – level 2
PC3 AT3 Writing   – level 2 (weighted 7)
PC3 AT4 Spelling   – level 1 (weighted 2)
PC3 AT5 Handwriting   – level 2 (weighted 1)
                        so PC3 =   level 2

Reported assessment for English: level 2.

It is interesting to note that similarity of subject level (Brent and Chris) may mask large within-subject differences. This has implications for the grouping of children, discussed in chapter 7.

Rules involving disapplications of AT

Circular 9/90 lays down precise rules concerning disapplications: 'For a pupil for whom an AT which constitutes a profile component in its own right is disapplied, it will not be possible to determine a level by profile component' (DES 1990g: Annex, para. 2a). Thus, a child who had, for example, 'speaking and listening' or 'reading' ATs disapplied could not be given a level on those targets.

> In the case of the writing component in English, no level should be determined in the event of the attainment target in writing being disapplied, and nor then should a level for the pupil in English be determined. A profile component and subject level will however be determined where the handwriting AT or spelling ATs have been disapplied using the rules and appropriate weightings set out in articles 7(4) and 7(5) of the Order.
>
> (DES 1990g: Annex, para. 2b)

English has three profile components (speaking and listening, reading and writing). The third of these, writing, is made up of three ATs (writing, spelling and handwriting). If the writing AT has been disapplied, then the child cannot be given a level on the writing profile component or for English as a whole. The writing AT is like a switch which must be set to 'on' (i.e. applied) to give an English assessment. Much work with children with difficulties in learning focuses on the development of speaking and listening. This would not be reflected in overall English AT level unless the child were also working on the writing AT. In practice it is unlikely that any of the ATs in English would be disapplied widely, as virtually all children could be working on the targets at some level, even if using alternative communication systems such as Makaton or Paget-Gorman. SEAC (1990b) envisaged that there will be few disapplications from summative assessments in any subject and stated that summative assessments should not be disapplied in isolation. That is, summative assessments should only be disapplied if the relevant POSs or ATs are also disapplied.

There are specific rules which are applied to combining ATs in order to obtain a profile component level in maths or science. The details are given in Circular 9/90 (DES 1990g) and the following examples illustrate the procedures.

Maths programme for Ayesha

PC1	AT1 Using/applying maths	– applied
PC1	AT2 Number	– applied
PC1	AT3 Number	– applied
PC1	AT4 Number	– applied
PC1	AT5 Number/algebra	– disapplied
PC1	AT6 Algebra	– disapplied
PC1	AT7 Algebra	– disapplied
PC1	AT8 Measures	– applied
PC2	AT9 Using/applying maths	– applied
PC2	AT10 Shape and space	– applied
PC2	AT11 Shape and space	– applied
PC2	AT12 Handling data	– applied
PC2	AT13 Handling data	– applied
PC2	AT14 Handling data	– disapplied

Assessment for Ayesha

PC1	AT1 Using/applying maths	– level 2
PC1	AT2 Number	– level 1
PC1	AT3 Number	– level 2
PC1	AT4 Number	– level 2
PC1	AT5 Number/algebra	– n/a
PC1	AT6 Algebra	– n/a
PC1	AT7 Algebra	– n/a
PC1	AT8 Measures	– level 2
PC2	AT9 Using/applying maths	– level 2
PC2	AT10 Shape and space	– level 3
PC2	AT11 Shape and space	– level 1
PC2	AT12 Handling data	– level 1
PC2	AT13 Handling data	– level 2
PC2	AT14 Handling data	– n/a

Different rules apply to profile components 1 and 2 because of the 'one third' rules about aggregation. If more than one-third of the ATs have been disapplied then one set of rules applies; if one-third, or fewer than one-third, have been disapplied then a different set of rules applies. In profile component 1, over one-third of the ATs have been disapplied for Ayesha. Thus, she should not be assigned an overall level for that profile component or for maths as a whole. Her care-givers should be told of levels reached on individual ATs and on profile component 2. In profile component 2, less than one-third of the ATs have been disapplied. Five ATs have been applied. The level for the profile component is the level reached, or exceeded by, at least half of the ATs. In Ayesha's case this means that she is at level 2 on profile component 2.

The calculation and implications are straightforward in this example but the application of these rules can lead to anomalies. These have implications for all children, not just those with difficulties in learning. One solution would be to report results by AT rather than by profile component. This would avoid complex, and sometimes misleading, combining of ATs into profile components and would be more comprehensible to a wider audience.

Combining SAT results with other teacher assessments

If there is no SAT assessment for a particular AT then the teacher assessment is reported. Not all English, maths and science ATs are included in the key stage 1 SAT. The summative assessment will be a combination of SAT and teacher assessments. The effect of this will be to give the teacher's assessments greater weight in those profile components which are only partly assessed through SATs. In theory, children could be exempted from the SAT part only of an assessment.

In general, within the AT, the SAT assessment takes precedence over the teacher assessment if these differ. Thus, when making an assessment of a child's level on writing, for example, if the SAT activity led to an assessment of level 2 but the teacher's assessment was that the child was at level 3, then the reported level would be level 2. This clearly emphasises the responsibility of the constructors and administrators of the SATs to make these as valid and reliable as possible. Teachers, as noted earlier, tend to under-estimate attainments of children with difficulties in learning so the bias towards SATs might work in those children's favour. Parents have the right to information about both SAT and teacher assessments and how these have been combined.

The timing of assessments to be combined into summative results varies. Formative teacher assessments over a key stage are to be summarised in the spring term of the last year of the key stage. The SATs assessments are to be carried out after this in the first half of the following (i.e. summer) term. This will have the effect of giving the SAT assessment greater prominence because it will be more 'up to date'. Consequently, formative assessments over the whole key stage risk being seen as an irrelevance to those summative assessments which are made through SATs. For example, the SAT assessment of reading will take precedence over other teacher assessments of reading. Consequently, the teacher's formative assessments of a child's reading, made over the whole key stage, and summarised in the spring of the reporting year, will, in most cases, be irrelevant to reported group results.

Moderation

If there is a clash between an SAT assessment and a teacher assessment, such that the two results would have given different results on a profile component, then a moderating procedure can be started. SEAC (1990b) stated that there should be 'an absolute minimum' of cases needing to be resolved outside the school. Moderation of summative assessments was an important aspect of the TGAT Report (DES/WO 1988a, 1988b) but this has been weakened and altered in focus in later documents. Focus has shifted from group moderation, in which teachers would look at, for example, work from the lowest 5 per cent of children across a range of classes and schools. The change in the focus of moderation means that the potential for raising teachers' expectations by comparing attainments of similar groups of children has been lost. This could have been particularly valuable in relation to children with relatively low attainments. Instead, emphasis is on individualised moderation to balance different assessments (i.e. SAT and teacher assessments) of individual children. Presumably, this will tend to be an issue when the SAT gives an unexpectedly low, rather than unexpectedly high, attainment level for a child. More specifically, it may raise issues about very able children. The SAT at key stage 1 is at levels 1, 2 and 3 only so this will create an artificial ceiling on children's attainments. Extending key stage 2 SATs to these children would enable higher levels to be included.

PUBLICATION OF REPORTED ASSESSMENTS

Whether or not children with difficulties in learning should be included in published summative assessments has been hotly debated. In December 1988, Angela Rumbold, then Education Minister, said in a parliamentary answer that children with special needs would be excluded from published, group results. *From Policy to Practice* (DES 1989d) reiterated this stance and implied that excluding these children from published lists would be encouraged:

> The approach which is being adopted is ... to modify the requirements to publish school-based information about results of assessments but still assess how pupils with special educational needs are doing. That way schools need have no fear that the overall picture of attainment for their pupils will suffer because children with special educational needs are included.
>
> (DES 1989d: para. 8.5)

One difficulty with this approach concerns the lack of clarity about which children are encompassed by the 'special educational needs' label. Does this include children with statements of SEN, children working with a school special needs co-ordinator, any child thought to have special needs and even 'gifted' children? Unless the category is clearly defined, practice will vary widely between schools and LEAs. Even if a relatively clear category is used, such as children with statements of SEN under the 1981 Education Act, enormous differences in statementing practice across LEAs will make for large regional variations in children included in group attainment data.

Excluding one set of children from group, published results has several further disadvantages. First, excluding a sub-group of children from summative assessments conveys an impression that those children are less important than others in the classroom. Second, excluding some children's attainments from group summative assessments distorts the national picture of the effects and effectiveness of the NC. The reported group assessments would reflect what happens to average and above average children in relation to NC attainments rather than what happens to all children in maintained schools. This is important because of the experimental nature of the NC:

What we are all engaged in is simply the first national-scale exercise in a project which is designed to be evolutionary. We will improve it as we go along. That is what it is about.

John McGregor (DES 1990h: 13)

The distortion of overall results could be mitigated to some extent by having two tiers of reported results, one 'public' set excluding children with SEN and one 'private' set, for government monitoring purposes, which includes all children involved in NC assessments. Although this would meet my earlier objection to a distortion in monitoring of the NC, it would be undesirable and undemocratic to be revealing publicly only part of the picture. To exclude results concerning children with SEN would also deprive care-givers of data to inform judgements about which schools might best help their children. It is conceivable that a school which 'did well' with children with learning difficulties would be popular. If 20 per cent of all children have SEN (DES 1978a) then presumably approximately 20 per cent of care-givers have an interest in how well schools do with these children.

More recently, the advice from SEAC to the DES (Mittler 1990) is that children with difficulties in learning should be included in published lists of attainment levels. Including all children in reported group assessments is consistent with the principle, advocated in the 1981 Education Act, of educational integration. It will avoid a situation in which some teachers may have been tempted to give less attention to some children with difficulties in learning just because their results were excluded from group lists. Teachers will have to confront issues about how they help children with difficulties in learning to overcome those difficulties.

Despite these advantages, advocacy of all-inclusive group results is a risky position to take for several reasons. It may discourage the integration of children from special into mainstream schools if those children are thought likely to lower the school's results. It may also encourage heads to find ways of excluding some children's results from the published lists. One way to do this would be to use temporary exceptions (see chapter 11) to take some children out of reported assessments at the ends of key stages. DES documents have stressed that heads should not do this but it is difficult to envisage how such advice could be enforced. Governing bodies will have a decisive role in determining whether or not published lists are comprehensive. The LEA must be informed of temporary exceptions (in LEA maintained schools) but does not have the power, except for certain renewals of exceptions, to prevent them.

Re-organising some teaching groups, so that children with learning difficulties appear in reported assessments for younger age groups, would be another way to manipulate published assessment lists. This would retain those children with learning difficulties in reported, group assessments but would be less likely to 'pull down' the school's results. However, the detrimental effects of this type of streaming have been discussed in chapter 7.

The most obvious way to take children out of the summative assessments is by writing this into a statement of SEN. A dramatic increase in the number of children being given a statement has already been reported by educational psychologists (Berliner 1990) and education officers (Pyke 1990). The rise may reflect financial incentives for heads, because of LMS and various budget formulae, to increase the number of statemented children in a school. It may also reflect the use of statements to exclude children from parts of the NC, particularly summative assessments. These issues about whether or not children with learning difficulties should be included in group summative assessments could be swept away by removing the obligation to publish these results (at key stages 2, 3 and 4). It seems unlikely that such a reversal of policy will occur but it is to be hoped that schools will resist pressures to publish group results when they do have the choice, that is, at the end of key stage 1. Most children, whether or not they have difficulties in learning, will be included in summative assessments. The following section examines ways in which SAT assessments can be carried out so that children's attainments are revealed rather than hidden.

CARRYING OUT SATS WITH CHILDREN WITH LEARNING DIFFICULTIES

If SATs are a good way of assessing what they aim to assess (valid) and would give similar results from day to day or for different assessors (reliable), then they should be accepted as useful adjuncts to formative teacher assessments. Their major strength would be in enabling wider comparisons to be made between work in one school and broader standards. This would be valuable for several reasons.

Work on school effectiveness (e.g. Mortimore *et al.* 1988, Tizard *et al.* 1988) has shown the wide differences between standards attained in schools in similar areas. In particular, it has been claimed that teachers often under-estimate children with learning difficulties, whether those children are in mainstream or special schools (e.g. Bennett *et al.* 1984, DES 1978b). It would be useful for teachers and others to know if, for example, expectations for scientific understanding were low when compared with schools having similar populations. Similarly, it would be encouraging to know that reading levels, for example, compared well with schools in similar areas.

At present, no formal reports of the piloting of SATs have been published, making any discussion of validity and reliability of the piloted tasks impossible. Anecdotal reports in the press have high-lighted the managerial difficulties in carrying out SATs and the overall impression has been of the problems rather than the advantages of SATs. However, some teachers have expressed positive views about SATS, referring, for example, to the chance that it gave them to analyse more deeply what was happening in group work. One reported reaction (Bates 1990b) was that the pilot SATs prevented children with difficulties in learning from showing what they could do.

One of the factors which might lead children with learning difficulties to 'under-achieve' on SATs, and so produce an invalid assessment, is the child's motivation. Differentiation by task may discourage children with learning difficulties. Those children are likely to feel more confident, and so do better, if given 'easy' tasks to begin with. If the child does not want to carry out a task then any apparent level of attainment on the task is likely to under-estimate what he or she can do. Children who find school-based learning difficult are likely to feel anxious in situations which appear to be unusual learning contexts. Their fear of failing may lead them to avoid new learning experiences rather than treating them as a challenge. Consequently, for those children it will be vital that SATs are, as recommended in the TGAT Report (DES/WO 1988a), consistent with usual classroom practice. There is a con-flict here between past and future practice, as in some schools and for some subjects (notably technology) NC recommendations are explicitly and deliberately a considerable extension of past practice. Consequently, SATs in those schools, at least in the short term, may not be consistent with what children have experienced.

The child's failure to understand what is expected or required may also limit his or her attainments. Much research in developmental psychology has shown the importance of the context in which the task is presented. Ask a child if there is more or less liquid when water is transferred from a short, fat glass to a tall, thin glass and many young children will answer wrongly that the tall, thin glass holds more water. But put that task into a meaningful context, such as transferring orange juice from a cracked, short, fat glass to an uncracked, tall, thin glass, and the child recognises that no change has taken place in the amount of liquid (Wood 1988). Children with learning difficulties may, through lack of confidence in learning, be particularly likely to be swayed by the irrelevant in contexts which lack 'common sense' for them.

The child's understanding of the wording of the task is also important. For example, if a child is given a set of objects and asked to 'Sort these into magnetic and non-magnetic materials', the child may be unable to do this because the word 'magnetic' is not understood. If the task is re-phrased, to 'Sort the objects into things which stick to the magnet and things which don't stick to the magnet', this removes the lexical problem of whether or not the child understands 'magnetic' but it introduces a distracting element because of the ambiguity of 'stick to'. In primary classes, 'stick to' is probably used more often to refer specifically to glueing things than to mean 'adhere to'. Consequently, the child with learning difficulties, seeing that he or she has not been supplied with glue, may do nothing and so 'fail' the task. There is another source of ambiguity in the phrasing of the initial question above, that is in the use of the word 'materials'. Whereas many primary children would understand that this is a general term for a variety of things, the child with learning difficulties may interpret 'materials' very specifically as 'fabrics'. This may lead the child to sort the objects into those which do or do not contain fabric. Both of these examples reflect a lack of ability to generalise terms and this may impede a child with learning difficulties. However, confusion over 'sticking' and 'materials' would not necessarily mean that the child failed to understand magnetism. Other children, more tuned into classroom language, will probably interpret the instruction as intended by the teacher.

Work on teacher language (e.g. Edwards and Westgate 1987) has shown how the subtle conventions of classroom discourse are different from talk found outside classrooms. For example, if a child gives an incorrect answer to a question, then teachers commonly repeat the question but without saying that the first answer is incorrect:

TEACHER	What day is it today, Sandy?
SANDY	Saturday
TEACHER	What day is it today, Nicky?
NICKY	Tuesday.
TEACHER	That's right, Tuesday. Swimming day.

Most children tune into these discourse conventions but children with difficulties in learning may not do so. They are more inclined to interpret what is happening at face value. For example, in the above example, they may not realise for some while that 'Saturday' was the incorrect answer because there was no specific feedback telling Sandy that it was incorrect. Conversely, children may be too ready to accept the convention that a repeated question means that the first answer was incorrect (Edwards and Mercer 1987). This is particularly so for a child who lacks confidence in his or her learning:

TEACHER	Does the bag of shells weigh more than the marble?
RACHEL	Yes.
TEACHER	Does the bag of shells weigh more than the marble?
RACHEL	No.

Teachers carrying out formal assessment procedures may be likely to repeat a question in order to be sure that they have understood the child's intended answer. That, as in the above extract, may confuse a child who lacks confidence and lead the child to 'correct' a right answer. Thus, there are various conventions of classroom language which become very significant when translated into an assessment context. The children who have failed to understand the conventions are not just naïve members of the class but also failing to do themselves justice on cognitive tasks.

The teacher's expectations may also limit a child's attainments. An extensive body of research has shown that children tend to work at the levels expected of them. Crudely, children labelled as 'slow learners' tend to behave in that way while children identified as high achievers live up to expectations. In the context of SATs this means that, in a wide range of subtle ways, the teacher may convey to the child that he or she is not expected to be able to carry out an activity. This includes giving the child a relatively short time in which to respond, allowing interruptions from other children, or not re-phrasing questions. This is important in the context of assessment and the NC because many of the SOAs are unclear and so judgements about attainments are open to bias by the assessor. Whether or not a child can 'copy, continue and devise repeating patterns' (Ma 5/1) may be fairly clear. Targets which concern 'knowing' are much harder to define categorically in terms of whether or not they have been attained. Knowing about something is a continuum in which the knower moves through various degrees of understanding. For example, to 'know that living things respond to seasonal and daily changes' (Sc 2/3c) could be understood with a wide range of varying degrees of sophistication. Imagine three children who, in conversation with the teacher, make the following comments in relation to this AT:

SUSIE   I always want to eat hot food in winter and ice-cream in summer.

WAYNE   Some animals hibernate in winter because food is hard to find then.

MELANIE   Some mammals, fish, reptiles and birds hibernate. In hibernation, body processes are slowed down. It is a natural process to help the animal to avoid dying because of heat loss, freezing or shortage of food.

Whether or not Susie is rated as having attained level 3 on this AT may depend in part on the teacher's expectations of Susie. If Susie is regarded by the teacher as of generally low ability, the response might count as below level 3 because it is self-referenced and lacks the detail given by the other two children. If the teacher holds higher expectations of Susie then her response may be classed as at level 3 because she has indicated a link between behaviour and seasonal changes.

Children who have difficulties in school-based learning are often described as having short concentration spans. Some SATs in the pilot work have entailed detailed and sustained work over one period. Some children may do poorly in such a situation, not because they are unable to complete the task but because they tend to work in short bursts and attention wanders over a longer period. Conversely, some children may need a relatively long time to complete an activity. If SATs are untimed then the teacher can allow for this. How SATs are managed in the class as a whole will have a bearing on whether or not the teacher can accommodate this. Some children might do better if they can carry out the longer SATs activities in a quiet area outside the classroom.

The child's relationship with the teacher who is giving the assessment task is also likely to influence how well the child does the task. One finding to emerge from psychological work on interview techniques has been the growing realisation of the influence of interviewer characteristics on the responses elicited. People respond differently to interviewers whom they like or dislike, who are of the same or opposite sex to themselves, who come from similar or contrasting backgrounds and who are of the same or a different ethnic group. Similarly, children with learning difficulties are likely to respond in very different ways to different teachers. The implication for SATs is that, ideally, schools need to give the child the best chance by careful choice of the adult(s) with whom the child works. In practice, it may be that this will always be the class teacher but there may be a case for using a support teacher to work through SATs with specific children.

There is strong and increasing evidence of the effect of age on school attainments (e.g. Mortimore *et al.* 1988, Tizard *et al.* 1988). Summer born children starting school in the Autumn following their fifth birthdays have one year less in the infant school compared with Autumn born children who start school at the beginning of the term in which their fifth birthdays fall. This means that at the end of key stage 1 some children may have had only two years in school (one third of their lives) while other children will have had three years (nearly half of their lives). The significance of this is evident from surveys showing that a disproportionate number of children with difficulties in learning are the younger (i.e. summer born) children in a year group. These children are not really less able than their classmates but just younger. In theory, SATs results could take this into account but it would require a complex standardisation of SATs (as happens for standardised reading tests which adjust raw scores for chronological age in years and months).

The method of presenting the task may also affect attainments. Reports of SATs for the end of key stage 1 indicate that they have avoided heavy reliance on reading. Consequently, a child who had poor reading levels could none the less demonstrate, for example, scientific understanding. This is likely to be a more critical issue for SATs at the end of key stage 2, where it may be assumed that all children have adequate reading levels for the task. Pressures of time to manage SATs, evident from the key stage 1 pilots, may lead designers of key stage 2 SATs to use more pencil and paper tasks because they will be seen as being quicker and more manageable than practical tasks. This would clearly be likely to hamper children with reading difficulties from demonstrating attainments in other areas. Where the written word is the medium through which an SAT is posed, then the SAT's focus is confounded with, not independent from, reading ability.

The significance (for schools and perhaps care-givers) of attainment on SATs will be greater than attainments on other, more routine, school tasks. Despite the emphasis in the TGAT Report (DES/WO 1988a), and in most of the pilot stage 1 SATs, on making the SATs part of normal classroom activities, it seems probable that children will pick up from teachers the relative seriousness of SATs activities. This could work in two ways: it might motivate some children but might increase anxiety for others (especially those with low academic self-esteem). Children with learning difficulties are likely to be in this latter group. Children who fail to note the significance of SATs may under-achieve because they quickly give up, lose interest or just prefer to do something else.

This discussion has highlighted various ways in which reported assessments at the ends of key stages may be invalid and unreliable, particularly in relation to children with learning difficulties. Some of these can only be overcome in the design of the SATs and revision of SATs should lead to greater validity and reliability. Other threats to validity and reliability may be overcome by the way in which the teacher carries out the activities. All of the factors which enhance motivation, such as where, when and with whom the activity is done, should be arranged to give the children the best chance of showing attainments. Many of the points which were made in chapter 6, concerning helping children to gain access to the NC, apply here. For example, some children may need to be told instructions rather than reading them independently or they may need more time for tasks than do other children.

This chapter was written in October 1990 and reflects the current knowledge concerning SATs. The chapter has tended to focus on possible barriers to obtaining useful information from SATs. It should be set in the context of the limitations of the

summative tests of children's attainments which have been used
prior to the NC. Many surveys attest to the widespread use of
out-of-date standardised tests which have little relationship to
classroom teaching. There are, potentially, advantages in SATs if
these are planned and carried out sensitively within a broader
assessment programme. It may be the case that teachers believe,
even so, that children with difficulties in learning are not doing
themselves justice in terms of attainments on SATs. If this is the
case it is important to collate the evidence to show this so that the
assessment process can be modified accordingly.

Chapter 11

Formal modifications and disapplications of the National Curriculum

The emphasis in the NC is that it is for all children in maintained schools (with the single exception of the small group of children in hospital special schools). It is not enough to have the NC available generally in a school. The NC, as described in the Orders, must be offered to every child in maintained schools unless modifications or disapplications have been made.

Given that this is the statutory position, one may ask if it is desirable that children with learning difficulties are, in principle, to be included in the NC? If the answer to this question is 'yes', then discussion of modifications and disapplications will focus on how to minimise these. However, as Jean Ware (1990) has argued in relation to children with severe learning difficulties it is conceivable that it would benefit children to be exempted, or freed, from the NC. In that case, discussion might focus on how to maximise disapplications and modifications. The stance taken in this book is that full participation in the NC is a desirable, initial goal for all children in mainstream schools.

There are many ways in which the NC might be adapted, for example, through helping children to gain access to the curriculum (discussed in chapters 5 and 6) or placing the child in a teaching group with younger children (see chapter 7). These ways are informal and do not require formal modifications. Such informal modifications slide into formal modifications and it is not clear when the former become the latter (Daniels and Ware 1990). Formal modifications or disapplications of the NC may be used in various situations, not exclusively for children with difficulties in learning.

PROCEDURES FOR FORMALLY MODIFYING OR DISAPPLYING THE NATIONAL CURRICULUM

There are five routes through which the NC may be modified or disapplied and these may be related to: children with statements of SEN; children with SEN who do not have statements; children who, through special circumstances such as prolonged illness, may none the less not receive the NC for a period of time (nominally up to six months); children, not necessarily having SEN, who are involved in development work.

'Disapplication' means that the child is not involved in specified parts of the NC. 'Modification' means that the NC, although the child will be 'doing' it, is altered in some way. Modifications might concern level and/or access (Norwich 1989). Modifications to the level at which a child is working might, for example, involve stipulating that the child, although he or she is at key stage 2 and theoretically should be working at levels 2–5 (or 6, depending on the subject area), may carry out work at level 1. Modifications of access might involve making clear in the statement that the child will use signing systems rather than oral communication.

1 Modification or disapplication through a statement of SEN

There are four elements in the NC: subjects, POSs, ATs (sub-divided into statements of attainment at each of ten levels) and assessment arrangements. A child's statement could specify disapplication or modification of any one or more of these aspects (ERA section 18). For example, a child might be exempted from certain foundation subjects in order to give more curriculum time for self-help skills. Alternatively, a child might follow all foundation subjects but not all ATs. If some ATs (say, algebra targets in mathematics) were disapplied then presumably the associated assessment arrangements for those targets would also be disapplied. It would be possible, although this is being discouraged, for a statement to disapply only part of the assessment arrangements; for example, to indicate that a child should follow all of the POSs and ATs in science but should not be included in summative assessments of science at the ends of key stages. This would be difficult to justify unless the summative assessments (e.g. the SATs element) were clearly inappropriate for these children. In theory, there should not be a disparity betweeen the nature of the POS and the nature of the assessment.

Any modification or disapplication in a child's statement of SEN must be accompanied by an account of what is to be offered as an alternative, bearing in mind that all pupils should receive a broad and balanced curriculum (DES 1989d). This leaves unanswered questions about what would be permissible within the ERA. Children with emotional and behavioural difficulties might need a curriculum heavily oriented to developing personal and social skills although, in the terms expressed in the ERA, this would break the statutory requirement for a broad and balanced curriculum.

It is not the case that a child with a statement of SEN will automatically have the NC disapplied or modified. For example, it would be feasible for only a few children in a school of primary-aged children with moderate learning difficulties to have the NC modified or disapplied, even though most of these children would have statements of SEN.

There has been a shift concerning advice about disapplying or modifying the NC through a child's statement. The draft of Circular 22/89 (DES 1988c) suggested that a statement might be required where no other means could be found to bring in a modification or disapplication (para. 30). Interestingly, this point was dropped from the final version of the Circular (DES 1989c). That Circular noted only that statements *may* not be needed where mainstream schools determine and make special educational provision from their own resources. The draft version could have had the effect of increasing the number of children with statements in mainstream schools (with the concommitant resource implications). Arguably, the final version, by explicitly excluding reference to using a statement to obtain disapplications or modifications, will lead instead to a greater use of 'directions', which do not contain the same statutory obligation to provide the necessary resources.

2   Disapplication or modification through a temporary 'direction'

A head teacher may temporarily disapply or modify the NC for a child for, initially, up to six months (ERA section 19). Temporary exceptions ('directions') are of two kinds: general directions and special directions.

General directions

General directions can be applied in a diverse range of circumstances including: pupils newly arrived from a different education system; pupils who have had some time in hospital, who have been educated at home or been excluded from school; pupils who temporarily have severe emotional problems; children who, for reasons other than these, have had extended absence from school (DES 1989e: para. 13). A head does not *have* to make general directions in these circumstances. General directions can also be given for a child who has a statement of SEN.

There are several categories for which general directions are not needed. These categories include: children away from school through illness or holidays, children who have been temporarily excluded from school, children concentrating for several weeks on areas in which they have particular weaknesses and children who are on the register of a school but receive part of their education elsewhere (DES 1989e).

The groups of children included in these two sets of categories are extremely confusing and it is difficult to envisage how these general directions can operate consistently and effectively in practice. There seems to be little logic in which groups may or may not be the subject of directions. It would have been more constructive to focus on ways in which the NC could genuinely meet the needs of all children, including those given as able to have temporary disapplications or modifications.

Special directions

The other category of temporary exceptions ('special directions') applies to children to cover the period during which they are 'being assessed for special educational needs' or statements of SEN are being prepared (DES 1989e: para. 19).

Procedures

The procedures for applying special directions are similar to the procedures for general directions and are summarised in table 11.1. Directions have to be made for individual pupils, not groups, so that a group direction could not be made, for example, on all of the children receiving extra reading support. Before giving a direction it is *expected* that the head will *consult*: the class teacher, the child's parent(s)/guardian(s), and specialist staff such as educational psychologists and medical officers. This consultation

Table 11.1 Summary table of procedures for making an initial direction

Schools	General directions	Special directions
LEA maintained		
Recommended consultation with:	Parents[1] Teachers Specialists	Parents[1] Teachers Specialists
Required consultation with:		LEA
Prior written consent in case of renewal from:	3 governors[2] LEA[3]	
Prior written consent in case of new direction[4] from:	LEA	3 governors LEA
Inform (in writing):	Parents[1] Chair of governors LEA	Parents[1] Chair of governors LEA
Grant-maintained		
Recommended consultation with:	Parents[1] Teachers Specialists	Parents[1] Teachers Specialists
Required consultation with:		LEA
Prior written consent in case of renewal from:	3 governors[2] LEA[2]	
Prior written concent in case of new direction[4] from:	3 governors	3 governors
Inform (in writing):	Parents[1] Chair of governors	Parents[1] Chair of governors LEA

[1] 'Parents' denotes at least one parent or guardian of the child, as registered at the school.
[2] If first and second renewal.
[3] Second renewal.
[4] Must be based on different reasons from previous direction.
Source: Regulations (1181, 1989) and accompanying Circular 15/89 (DES 1989e)

is expected, but not mandatory, and this has been criticised as diminishing the importance of, in particular, liaison with parents (Russell 1990). Once a general or special direction has been made, the head must, within three working days, inform in writing: at least one of the child's parent(s)/guardian(s) (as registered at the school), the chair of the school governing body and the LEA (if the school is LEA maintained). Where the parents or guardians have difficulty in understanding a direction, the head should make appropriate arrangements to explain what is planned, for example, by providing a translation (written or oral) of the direction.

The head must generally allow one month before the direction comes into force, although in exceptional cases it can be brought in more quickly. This is to give parents and the LEA (for LEA maintained schools) time to query the proposed direction. The direction must include the following information: which type of direction is being applied, why the action is being taken, what type of action is being taken, and what alternatives to the NC are being offered (these must be 'positive alternatives'). In addition, for a general direction, the head must specify: why present circumstances prevent the child from receiving the NC, how these circumstances seem likely to change over the period of the direction (i.e. the next six months [or less]), and how the child will be brought back into the NC. If a child who is the subject of a general or special direction leaves the school, then the direction ceases to apply. The head of the child's new school would have to decide whether or not a new direction is needed. Directions can be transferred from one head of a school to his or her successor.

Varying or revoking a direction

If a general direction has been brought in because, for example, a child has been in hospital, this direction might well be nominally for six months (it could be for a shorter period). However, if after, say, three months it is decided that there is no need for the direction to continue then the head could revoke or change the direction. The procedures for informing relevant individuals of an initial direction apply again when giving information about changing or withdrawing the direction.

One possible type of variation of a direction within a six monthly period would be for a child attending a unit away from the school for a short period. For example, a general direction might be used to enable a child to attend a reading support unit in an LEA centre for two terms (e.g. January–June) but one term might turn out to be sufficient or, because of pressure on unit places, the child attends for only one term. Then the head would have to amend the initial direction to show that the child returned to the home school full-time after (say) three, not six months. If the head withdraws a direction then he or she must state the reasons for this, when it is to take effect and how the child is to be re-integrated into the NC.

Renewing directions.

General directions can be renewed by the head, firstly for a further three months (provided that written consent is obtained from three school governors). The renewal has to follow the initial direction, so that a head could not bring in a temporary direction for (e.g.) January–June, let it lapse over July–August and then 'renew' the initial direction in September. A second renewal of the initial direction is possible for a further three months, so that heads can, in effect, bring in a temporary exemption from the NC for twelve months. However, the second three-monthly renewal has to be agreed both with three school governors and (for LEA maintained schools) with the LEA. A broadly similar situation applies to renewing special directions. In all types of renewals of directions, the same consultative processes as were outlined when making the initial direction are expected to take place.

A head cannot bring in any further general directions for an individual child after this maximum twelve-month direction unless different reasons are given. Thus it would be possible to make general directions disapplying or modifying the NC for up to twelve months on the basis of a child's learning difficulties and then bring in a new set of directions based on the child's emotional difficulties. Making a second direction on a child requires prior written consent of three school governors and (for LEA maintained schools) the LEA.

The system, while apparently trying to meet the possible needs of individual children, is open to abuse. The misuse of temporary exceptions, for example, a casual and excessive use of them in order to remove 'difficult' children from the system, was recognised by the DES. Amendments to the draft circular on temporary exceptions were made in order to 'lay added emphasis on the intention that the powers of direction should be used sparingly' and it was stated that, 'the Secretary of State will be monitoring the powers of direction' (DES 1989e: annex A). It is not clear what action would be taken, or by whom, against a school which appeared to be 'over-applying' directions.

3   Orders issued by the Secretary of State

Orders have been made by the Secretary of State under section 4 of the ERA to disapply or modify the NC for certain groups of children. The Orders for some of the individual subjects include amended ATs for children with specific types of learning difficulties. For example, the Orders for English key stage 1, ATs 1–4, include notes to the effect that pupils with various difficulties (e.g. poor speech, hearing or visual impairment) may use alternative methods of communication such as braille or signing systems. AT 5, handwriting, may be excluded for children who use braille (or similar systems) and children with such physical disabilities that even level 1 of the handwriting AT is unattainable.

Science POSs include similar flexibility. For example, the POS for key stage 1 includes work on observation. A footnote indicates that 'observe' is taken to mean 'to observe or consciously notice, by whatever means, using any of the senses' (DES/WO 1989a: 66). Similarly, AT 13/1b states: 'Pupils should be able to describe by talking, *or other appropriate means* , how food is necessary for life' (DES/WO 1989a: 28; my emphasis).

4   Regulations issued by the Secretary of State

Groups of children with learning difficulties, with or without statements, may also be exempt from the NC through regulations issued by the Secretary of State (ERA section 17). It would be feasible for, say, children with severe learning difficulties to be exempted from (e.g.) a foreign language by means of group regulations, although to date no such regulations have been applied to children with learning difficulties. Klaus Wedell (1990) reported only one instance of these regulations and this was in relation to pupils who attain level 10 before age 16.

5   Exemption from NC through development work

The ERA (section 16) specifies that children in a particular school may have the NC disapplied or modified for development work or experiments to be carried out.

PARENTS' RIGHTS CONCERNING FORMAL
DISAPPLICATIONS AND MODIFICATIONS

Parents (or guardians) can make a request, initially to the head
and then to the school governors, that the NC be disapplied or
modified. Similarly, parents can request that a disapplication or
modification be changed and that their child be brought back into
the NC. Parents do not have the power to remove their child from
the NC while the child is educated within the state system. It is
preferable if such requests can be discussed and resolved
informally between the head and the parents but regulations on
temporary exemptions from the NC (DES 1989e) lay down very
specific procedures if informal discussions do not resolve the issue.
In this situation, parents must then put their request in writing to
the head. The head has to consider changing a direction once only
during the course of that direction, so that parents could, for
example, expect a reply from their first request that one
six-monthly direction be changed. However, if the parents
continued to write (e.g. every month), then the head would not be
bound by law to reply to these subsequent requests. Similarly, the
head has to reply to only one such request during any one renewal.

Once the written request has been made by the parents, the
head must reply within two weeks. If the head disagrees with the
parents' request, then the head has to write to the parents, to the
governing body and (if an LEA maintained school) to the LEA,
explaining his or her reasons. If the head agrees with the parents
then clearly appropriate action is set in motion. If the parents do
not hear from the head in writing within two weeks of their
request, or if the head turns it down, then the parents can take the
request to the governing body. Circular 15/89 on temporary
exceptions advises that governors should deal 'with all due speed'
(DES 1989e: para. 6, annex B) with such appeals. To help
governors to respond quickly to parental requests concerning the
NC, any member of the governing body (except the head) or any
committee of governors can hear the appeal. The governors have
three options. They can decide to agree with the head, agree with
the parents, or 'take any other action they consider appropriate
within the scope of the regulations' (DES 1989e: para. 8, annex B).
The head teacher must comply with the governors' decision.

These procedures place a lot of power in the hands of possibly
inexperienced governors and have implications for governor

training in LEAs. They also make the role of the SEN co-ordinator very important, in relation to informing and advising school governors about special needs work and resources in the school, (see chapter 8). Regulations concerning parental appeals under the 1981 Education Act remain and are slightly strengthened as parents must now be informed in writing of any revision to a child's statement.

This chapter has reviewed formal procedures for disapplying or modifying the NC. The heavy statutory emphasis on these procedures sits uneasily alongside the rhetoric of the NC which stresses its suitability for all children. If the NC is really attuned to individuals' learning needs then there should be no cause for any disapplications or modifications. The cumbersome mechanisms surrounding exceptions can be seen as indicators of the limitations of the overall design of the NC. Exceptions will be important in shaping reform of the NC. For example, if modifications and disapplications emerge as invariably relating to the need for more personal and social education (PSE), this will indicate a need to include PSE more substantially and explictly within the NC.

Chapter 12

Conclusion: a glimpse ahead

Ian McEwan has written in the preface to *A Move Abroad*, of the changes in Britain in the 1980s:

> In a very short time, Great Britain began to feel like a quite different place as this new spirit took hold. Money-obsessed, aggressively competitive and individualistic, contemptuous of the weak, vindictive towards the poor, favouring the old American opposition of private affluence and public squalor, and individual gain against communal solutions, indifferent to the environment, deeply philistine, enamoured of policemen, soldiers and weapons: virile times indeed.
>
> (McEwan 1989: XXIV)

Is Ian McEwan right in this view? Objectively quantifying a 'new spirit' is hazardous. How does one prove that attitudes really have changed and in the direction that he suggests? This can be assessed quantitatively, measured by items such as the proportion of income given to charity, or perceptually, measured by such means as people's impressions of the likelihood of being the victim of crime. Perceptions are not necessarily in line with reality but they none the less have an important influence on how people behave. Elderly women fear crime more than do other groups and this deters many older women from going out alone after dark, whereas young men are less fearful but are more likely to suffer street attacks. Similarly, perceptions about education are an important determinant of how teachers work, even if these perceptions differ from the reality.

Fred Sedgwick (1989) has written vividly of how political influences on education have affected his work as head of a primary school. He echoes many of Ian McEwan's sentiments and concludes bluntly:

> Educational reform is being used to increase social divisions ...
> I have written with a confessed belief that ... teachers have a duty
> to offer the best, regardless of ephemera like what is cost
> effective in the market place of the late 1980s'.
>
> (Sedgwick 1989: 151–152).

The NC has generated enormous debate about the school curriculum and that is to be welcomed because discussion brings into the open unspoken assumptions about the nature and purposes of education.

There are strengths in the NC that can be built on for the benefit of all children, including those who have difficulties in learning. A shared curriculum in terms of aims and some content, but differentiation of approaches; the emphases on maintaining continuity, curricular breadth, coherence, progression and high expectations are all valuable aspects of the NC. Nevertheless, many commentators (e.g. Daniels and Ware 1990, Kelly 1990) have concluded that changes embodied in the ERA presage a diminishing in the quality of education offered to children with difficulties in learning. It must be right to alert others to weaknesses and anomalies in the ERA, and the NC specifically, but if pessimism takes hold then apprehensions may turn into self-fulfilling prophesies. This is particularly so in relation to the educational integration of children from special schools into mainstream settings. We are in danger of creating two more educational myths: that pre-ERA, integration flourished and that post-ERA, it became impossible. The second myth is the more dangerous now because it may deter teachers from even contemplating further integration.

The results of the implementation of the NC are unpredictable, not least because the teachers who will be operating the NC will, on past evidence, find all manner of ways to adjust it to their own beliefs if they, like Fred Sedgwick, are unhappy about its anticipated effects. Even if all teachers follow the NC as laid down in the Orders, we still cannot say with any certainty what the outcome will be. Naturalists, aiming to preserve a rare butterfly, fenced off part of its breeding ground to protect the delicate host plants from sheep grazing in the area. As a result, the grass in the protected area grew vigorously, smothering the host plants. The butterflies lost the plants on which they laid their eggs and so the careful protection led not to the hoped for increase in butterfly numbers but to their extinction. The moral is that all of the elements of the system need to be considered.

Does the ERA consider all of the elements in the system? Of course, it does not and it would be impossible for it to do so. Perhaps in focusing on the NC framework of subjects, POSs and assessment arrangements we shall stunt educational opportunities while ostensibly enriching them. The ERA, and the NC within it, are policies in which many elements are uncontrolled. In this light it is understandable that John MacGregor (DES 1990h) emphasised the experimental nature of the NC.

Complex systems are not readily manipulated; unforeseen outcomes, positive and negative, may result. While good intentions may have disastrous results, they may also have effects which are beneficial but not those which were intended. Post-it notes, with their strips of semi-adhesive 'glue', are said to be the result of a development which went wrong. The glue was insufficiently sticky but instead of a failed product the company had a new and (now) seemingly indispensable item for the school, office or home. The NC may also have consequences which are far from those intended by its constructors. For example, tighter monitoring of attainments may lead to questioning about resources rather than teaching quality. Disapplications and modifications for children with difficulties in learning may point to weaknesses in the curriculum for all children. The limits of the NC will be demonstrated by establishing how far it can meet educational aims for all children.

References

ACE (Advisory Centre for Education) (1989) 'Exceptions to the rule', Bulletin no. 32, November–December, London: ACE

ACE/AGIT (Advisory Centre for Education/Action for Governors Information and Training) (1990) *Governors and Special Educational Needs*, Conference Report, Manchester Polytechnic, March.

Ainscow, M. and Florek, A. (eds) (1989) *Special Educational Needs: Towards a Whole School Approach*, London: David Fulton/NCSE.

Ainscow, M. and Muncey, J. (1984) *Special Needs Action Programme* (SNAP), Cardiff: Drake/Coventry Local Education Authority.

Ainscow, M. and Tweddle, D. (1979) *Preventing Classroom Failure: An Objectives Approach*, London: Wiley.

Ainscow, M. and Tweddle, D. (1984) *Early Learning Skills Analysis* (ELSA), London: Wiley.

Allen, V.L. (1976) *Children as Teachers*, New York: Academic Press.

Alston, J. and Taylor, J. (1987) *Handwriting: Theory, Research and Practice*, London: Croom Helm.

Archer, M. (1989) 'Targeting change', *Special Children* 33, 14–15.

Arnold, H. (1982) *Listening to Children Reading*, London: Hodder and Stoughton/UKRA.

Ashdown, R., Carpenter, B. and Bovair, K. (eds) (1991) *The Curriculum Challenge: Pupils with Severe Learning Difficulties and the National Curriculum*, Lewes: Falmer.

Avann, P. (1985) *Teaching Information Skills in the Primary School*, London: Arnold.

Baker, D. and Bovair, K. (eds) (1989) *Making the Special Schools Ordinary*, Lewes: Falmer.

Barsby, J. (1991) 'Self-evaluation and seven year olds', *Education 3–13* 19: 1, 12–17.

Bastiani, J. (ed.) (1987) *Parents and Teachers 1: Perspectives on Home–School Relations*, Windsor: NFER/Nelson.

Bates, S. (1990a) 'Magnetic pull and push', *Guardian*, 16 January, p. 21.

Bates, S. (1990b) 'Teachers condemn primary school tests', Guardian, 25 June.

Beard, R. (1987) *Developing Reading 3–13*, London: Hodder and Stoughton.

Beck, K. (1989) 'Parental involvement in school: some dilemmas',

Education 3–13, 17: 3 101–2.

Beech, J.R. and Harding, L. (eds) (1991) *Educational Assessment in the Primary School*, Windsor: NFER/Nelson.

Behrmann, M. (1985) *Handbook of Micro-computers in Special Education*, Windsor: NFER/Nelson.

Bell, G.H. and Colbeck, B. (1989) *Experiencing Integration: The Sunnyside Action Enquiry Project*, Lewes: Falmer.

Bennett, N. and Cass, A. (1989) *From Special to Ordinary Schools: Case Studies in Integration*, London: Cassell.

Bennett, N. and Kell, A. (1989) *A Good Start?*, Oxford: Blackwell.

Bennett, N., Desforges, C., Cockburn, A. and Wilkinson, B. (1984) *The Quality of Pupil Learning Experiences*, London: Lawrence Erlbaum Associates.

Berliner, W. (1990) '"Special needs" schools ploy', *Independent*, 22 July.

Blatchford, P. (1989) *Playtime in the Primary School*, Windsor: NFER/Nelson.

Blyth, C.A. and Wallace, F.M.S. (1988) 'An investigation into the difficulties of transferring written records from the nursery school to the primary school', *Educational Research* 30: 3 219–23.

Bossert, S. (1987) 'Classroom task organisation and children's friendships', pp. 133–49 in A. Pollard (ed.) *Children and their Primary Schools*, Lewes: Falmer.

Bruce, T. (1987) *Early Childhood Education*, London: Hodder and Stoughton.

Bryant, P. and Bradley, L. (1985) *Children's Reading Problems*, Oxford: Blackwell.

CACE (1967) *Children and their Primary Schools*, London: HMSO.

Calderhead, J. (ed.) 1988) *Teachers' Professional Learning*, Lewes: Falmer.

Carpenter, B. and Lewis, A. (1989) 'Searching for solutions: A curriculum for integration of SLD and PMLD children', pp. 103–124 in D. Baker and K. Bovair (eds) *Making the Special Schools Ordinary?*, Lewes: Falmer.

Carpenter, B., Lewis, A. and Moore, J. (1986) 'An integration project involving young children with severe learning difficulties and mainstream first school children', *Mental Handicap*, 14: 4 152–7.

Carpenter, B., Fathers, J., Lewis, A. and Privett, R. (1988) 'Integration: The Coleshill experience', *British Journal of Special Education* 15: 3, 119–21.

Christie, T. (1990) 'Address to the National Primary Conference', Scarborough, reported in *Junior Education*, 9 June.

Clark, M.M., Barr, J.E. and Dewhirst, W. (1984) *Early Education of Children with Communication Problems: particularly those from ethnic minorities*, Offset publication no. 3, Birmingham: University of Birmingham.

Cleave, S., Jowett, S. and Bate, M. (1982) *And So to School*, Windsor: NFER/Nelson.

Crocker, A.C. and Cheeseman, R.G. (1988) 'The ability of young children to rank themselves for academic ability', *Educational Studies* 14: 1, 105–10.

Croft, P. (1989) 'The practice papers: resourcing the curriculum', *Special Children* 34, 1–4 November.

Croll, P. (1986) *Systematic Classroom Observation*, Lewes: Falmer.

Croll, P. and Moses, D. (1985) *One in Five*, London: Routledge.

Cronbach, L.J. and Snow, R.E. (1977) *Abilities and Instructional Methods*, New York: Irvington.

Daniels, H. and Ware, J. (1990) (eds) *Special Educational Needs and the National Curriculum*, Bedford Way Series, London: Kogan Page/Institute of Education, University of London.

Darnbrough, A. and Kinrade, D. (1985) *Directory for Disabled People*, 4th ed., London: RADAR/Woodhead-Faulkner.

David, T. and Lewis, A. (1991) 'Assessment in the reception class', in J.R. Beech and L. Harding (eds) *Educational Assessment in the Primary School*, Windsor: NFER/Nelson.

Dawson, R. (1985) *TIPS*, London: Macmillan Education.

DES (1978a) *Special Educational Needs* (Warnock Report), London: HMSO.

DES (1978b) *Primary Education in England*, London: HMSO.

DES (1982) *Mathematics Counts* (Cockcroft Report), London: HMSO.

DES (1985) *The Curriculum from 5–16*, Curriculum Matters 2 (HMI series), London: HMSO.

DES (1986) *A Survey of Science in Special Education*, HMI report, London: DES.

DES (1987) *The National Curriculum 5–16: A consultation document*, London: DES.

DES (1988a) *The New Teacher in School*, London: HMSO.

DES (1988b) *1987 Primary School Staffing Survey*, London: DES.

DES (1988c) 'Assessments and statements of special educational needs within the Education, Health and Social Services', Draft of Circular 22/89, London: DES/DH.

DES (1989a) *The Education Reform Act 1988: The School Curriculum and Assessment* Circular 5/89, London: HMSO.

DES (1989b) *The Education Reform Act 1988: National Curriculum: Mathematics and Science Orders under Section 4*, Circular 6/89, London: HMSO.

DES (1989c) *Assessments and statements of Special Educational Needs: procedures within the Education, Health and Social Services*, Circular 22/89, London: HMSO.

DES (1889d) *From Policy to Practice*, London: DES.

DES (1989e) *The Education Reform Act 1988: Temporary Exceptions from the National Curriculum*, Circular 15/89, London: HMSO.

DES (1990a) *Management of the School Day*, Circular 7/90, London: HMSO.

DES (1990b) *The Education Reform Act 1988: National Curriculum: English Stages Two to Four Order under Section 4*, Circular 2/90, London: HMSO.

DES (1990c) *The Education Reform Act 1988: National Curriculum Section 4 Order; Technology: Design and Technology and Information Technology*, Circular 3/90, London: HMSO.

DES (1990d) *History for ages 5 to 16*, London: HMSO.

DES (1990e) 'Staffing for pupils with special educational needs', Draft Circular, London: DES.

DES (1990f) *Records of Achievement*, Circular 8/90, London: HMSO.

DES (1990g) *The Education Reform Act 1988: The Education (National Curriculum) (Assessment Arrangements for English, Mathematics and Science) Order 1990*, Circular 9/90, London: HMSO.

DES (1990h) *National Curriculum and Assessment: Speeches on Education*, London: HMSO.

Dessent, T. (1987) *Making the Ordinary School Special*, Lewes: Falmer.

DES/WO (1988a) *National Curriculum: Task Group on Assessment and Testing* (TGAT Report), London: HMSO.

DES/WO (1988b) *National Curriculum: Task Group on Assessment and Testing, Three Supplementary Reports*, London: HMSO.

DES/WO (1989a) *Science in the National Curriculum*, London: HMSO.

DES/WO (1989b) *Mathematics in the National Curriculum*, London: HMSO.

DES/WO (1989c) *English for ages 5 to 16* (Cox Report) London: HMSO.

DES/WO (1990a) *Geography for ages 5 to 16*, London: HMSO.

DES/WO (1990b) *English in the National Curriculum*, London: HMSO.

DES/WO (1990c) *Technology in the National Curriculum*, London: HMSO.

Docking, J. (ed.) (1990) *Education and Alienation in the Junior School*, Lewes: Falmer.

Dyson, A. (1990) 'Effective learning consultancy: a future role for special needs coordinators?', *Support for Learning* 5: 3, 116–27.

Edwards, A.D. and Westgate, D.P.G. (1987) *Investigating Classroom Talk*, Lewes: Falmer.

Edwards, D. and Mercer, N. (1987) *Common Knowledge*, London: Methuen.

Elbaz, F. (1983) *Teacher thinking: a study of practical knowledge*, New York: Nichols.

Emblem, B. and Conti-Ramsden, G. (1990) 'Towards level 1: Reality or Illusion?' *British Journal of Special Education* 17: 3, 88–90.

Evans, L. (1989) 'Small steps to success: Resource pack', *Special Children* 35, 2–5 (inset).

Evans, P. and Varma, V. (eds) (1990) *Special Education: Past, Present and Future*, Lewes: Falmer.

EYCG (Early Years Curriculum Group) (1989) *Early Childhood Education: The Early Years Curriculum and the National Curriculum*, Stoke on Trent: Trentham Books.

Flude, M. and Hammer, M. (eds) (1990) *The Education Reform Act 1988: Its origins and implications*, Lewes: Falmer.

Gagné, R.M. (1968) 'Learning hierarchies', *Educational Psychology* 6: 1, 3–6.

Galton, M., Simon, B. and Croll, P. (1980 *Inside the Primary Classroom*, London: Routledge.

Gipps, C., Gross, H. and Goldstein, H. (1987) *Warnock's Eighteen Per Cent: Children with Special Needs in Primary Schools*, Lewes: Falmer.

Glynn, T. (1985) 'Contexts for independent learning', *Educational Psychology* 5: 1, 5–15.

Goacher, B., Evans, J., Welton, J. and Wedell, K. (1988) *Policy and Provision for Special Educational Needs*, London: Cassell.

Gurney, P. (1990) 'The enhancement of self-esteem in junior classrooms', pp. 7–24 in J. Docking (ed.) *Education and Alienation in the Junior School*, Lewes: Falmer.

Hanko, G. (1985) *Special Needs in Ordinary Classrooms*, Oxford: Blackwell.

Hargreaves, D.H., Hopkins, D., Leask, M., Connolly, J. and Robinson, P. (1989) *Planning for School Development Plans: Advice to Governors, Headteachers and Teachers*, London: DES.

Haring, N. G., Lovitt, T.C., Eaton, M.D. and Hansen, C.L. (1978) *The Fourth R: Research in the Classroom*, Columbus, OH: Merrill.

Haviland, J. (1988) *Take Care, Mr Baker!*, London: Fourth Estate.

Heaton, P. and Winterson, P. (1986) *Dealing with Dyslexia*, Bath: Better Books.

Hegarty, S. (1987) *Meeting Special Needs in Ordinary Schools*, London: Cassell.

Henderson, A. (1989) 'Multi-sensory maths', *Special Children* 33, 7–9.

Herbert, D. and Davies-Jones, G. (1984) *A Classroom Index of Phonic Resources*, Stafford: NARE.

Hirst, P. (1974) *Knowledge and the Curriculum*, London: Routledge and Kegan Paul.

HMI (1989a) *The implementation of the National Curriculum in Primary Schools*, London: DES.

HMI (1989b) *A Survey of Pupils with Special Educational Needs in Ordinary Schools*, London: DES.

HMI (1989c) *A survey of support services for special educational needs*, London: DES.

HMI (1990a) *Education Observed: Special Needs Issues*, London: HMSO.

HMI (1990b) *Standards in Education*, London: DES.

HMI (1990c) *Provision for Primary aged Pupils with Statements of Special Educational Needs in Mainstream Schools*, London: DES.

HMI (1990d) *The implementation of the National Curriculum in Primary schools: A survey of 100 schools*, London: DES.

Hofkins, D. (1990) 'SATs machinery stripped down', *Times Educational Supplement*, 26 October.

House of Commons; Education, Science and Arts Committee (1987) *Special Educational Needs: Implementation of the Education Act 1981*, Third Report from the Education, Science and Arts Committee Session 1986–87, vols. 1 and 2, London: HMSO.

Hughes, M. (1986) *Children and Number*, Oxford: Blackwell.

Hunter-Carsch, M. (1990) 'Learning strategies for pupils with literacy difficulties: motivation, meaning and imagery', pp. 222–36 in P.D. Pumfrey and C.D. Elliott (eds) *Children's Difficulties in Reading, Spelling and Writing*, Lewes: Falmer.

ILEA (1985a) *Educational Opportunities for All*, London: ILEA.

ILEA (1985b) *Improving Primary Schools*, London: ILEA.

Jones, G., Cato, V., Hargreaves, M. and Whetton, C. (1989) *Touchstones: Cross-curricular group assessments*, Windsor: NFER/Nelson.

Jones, N. and Frederickson, N. (eds) (1990) *Refocusing Educational Psychology*, Lewes: Falmer.

Jowett, S., Hegarty, S. and Moses, D. (1988) *Joining Forces*, Windsor: NFER/Nelson.

Kelly, V. (1990) *The National Curriculum: a critical review*, London: Paul Chapman.

King, V. (1989) 'The practice papers: Support teaching', *Special Children*, October 33, 1–4.

Lawton, D. and Chitty, C. (1988) *The National Curriculum*, Bedford Way Paper 33, London: University of London, Institute of Education.

Leclerc, M. (1985) *Classroom Aids, Apparatus and Materials*, Stafford: NARE.

Leicestershire LEA (1989) *Key Stages*, Leicester LEA.

Levey, B. and Branwhite, T. (1987) *The Precision Phonics Programme*, Stafford: NARE.

Lewis, A. (1983) 'A practical approach to the organisation of mathematics resources', Stafford, *NARE INSET 3*.

Lewis, A. (1985) 'Information Skills for Children with Learning Difficulties', pp. 27–42 in P. Avann (ed.) *Teaching Information Skills in the Primary School*, London: Arnold.

Lewis, A. (1988) 'Children with Special Needs in Primary Schools', pp. 123–40 in M. Clarkson (ed.) *Emerging Issues in Primary Education*, Lewes: Falmer.

Lewis, A. (1990) 'Six and seven year old "normal" children's talk to peers with severe learning difficulties', *European Journal of Special Needs Education* 5: 1, 21–30.

Lewis, A. (1991) 'Entitled to learn together?' in R. Ashdown, B. Carpenter and K. Bovair (eds) *The Curriculum Challenge: Pupils with Severe Learning Difficulties and the National Curriculum*, Lewes: Falmer.

Lewis, A. and Carpenter, B. (1990) 'Discourse, in an integrated school setting, between non-handicapped six and seven year olds and peers with severe learning difficulties', pp. 270–8 in W.I. Fraser (ed.) *Key Issues in Mental Retardation*, London: Routledge.

Lewis, A. and Thorpe, L. (1989) 'Planning cross-curricular work within the National Curriculum, for children with learning difficulties'. *Special Children: Primary Special*, 5–7.

Lloyd-Jones, R. (1985) *How to produce Better Worksheets*, London: Hutchinson.

McBrien, J. and Weightman, J. (1980) 'The effect of room management procedures on the engagement of profoundly retarded children', *British Journal of Mental Subnormality* 26: 1, 38–46.

McEwan, I. (1989) *A Move Abroad*, London: Picador.

Male, J. and Thompson, C. (1985) *The Educational Implications of Disability*, London: RADAR (Royal Association for Disability and Rehabilitation).

Meadows, S. and Cashdan, A. (1988) *Helping Children Learn*, London: David Fulton.

Mittler, P. (1990) 'The National Curriculum: an entitlement for all', Address to ACE/AGIT seminar on governors and special educational needs, Manchester, March.

Moore, J. and Morrison, N. (1988) *Someone Else's Problem? Teacher development to meet special educational needs*, Lewes: Falmer.

Moore J., Carpenter, B. and Lewis, A. (1987) '"He can do it really": Integration in a First School', *Education 3–13* 15: 2, 37–43.

Mortimore, P., Sammons, P., Stoll, L., Lewis, D. and Ecob, R. (1988) *School Matters*, Wells: Open Books.

Moses, D. (1982) 'Special educational needs: the relationship between teacher assessment, test scores and classroom behaviour', *British Journal of Educational Research* 8: 2, 111–22.

NCC (1989a) *Implementing the National Curriculum: participation by pupils with special educational needs*, Circular no. 5, York: NCC.

NCC (1989b) *The National Curriculum and whole curriculum planning: preliminary guidance*, Circular no. 6, York: NCC.

NCC (1989c) *A Framework for the Primary Curriculum*, York: NCC.

NCC (1989d) *A Curriculum for All*, York: NCC.

NCC (1989e) *NCC News*, December, York: NCC.

NCC (1989f) *An Introduction to the National Curriculum*, York: NCC.

NCC (1990a) *The Whole Curriculum*, York: NCC.

NCC (1990b) *NCC News*, April, York: NCC.

Nias, J. (1989) *Primary Teachers Talking*, London: Routledge.

Norwich, B. (1989) 'How should we define exceptions?', *British Journal of Special Education* 16: 3, 94–7.

Norwich, B. (1990) 'Decision making about special educational needs', pp. 34–49 in P. Evans and V. Varma (eds) *Special Education: Past, Present and Future*, Lewes: Falmer.

Nuttall, D. (1988) 'The implications of National Curriculum assessments', *Educational Psychology* 8: 4, 229–36.

Nuttall, D. (1989) 'National Assessement: will reality match aspirations?', *Education Section Review, British Psychological Society* 13: 1–2, 6–19.

Nuttall, D. and Goldstein, H. (1989) 'Finely measured gains', *Times Educational Supplement*, 27 October.

O'Toole, B. and O'Toole, P. (1989) 'How accessible is level 1 maths?', *British Journal of Special Education* 16: 3, 115–17.

Peters, M. (1975) *Diagnostic and Remedial Spelling Manual*, London: Macmillan.

Pollard, A. (1987) *Children and their Primary Schools*, Lewes: Falmer.

Pumfrey, P.D. and Elliott, C.D. (eds) (1990) *Children's Difficulties in Reading, Spelling and Writing*, Lewes: Falmer.

Pyke, N. (1990) 'Cuts blamed for rise in special needs referrals', *Times Educational Supplement*, 21 September.

RDAMP (The 1981 Education Act: Research Dissemination and Management Project) (1989) *Developing Services for Children with Special Educational Needs*, Loughborough: Tecmedia.

Reason, R. and Boote, R. (1986) *Learning difficulties in reading and writing: a Teacher's Manual*, Windsor: NFER/Nelson.

RNID (Royal National Institute for the Deaf) (1970) *Hearing Test Cards*, London: RNID.

Russell, P. (1990) 'The Education Reform Act: the implications for special educational needs', pp. 207–24 in M. Flude and M. Hammer (eds) *The Education Reform Act 1988: Its origins and implications*, Lewes: Falmer.

Rutter, M. and Yule, W. (1975) 'The concept of specific reading retardation', *Journal of Child Psychology and Psychiatry* 16, 181–97.

SEAC (1989) *National Curriculum Assessment Arrangements*, London: SEAC.

SEAC (1990a) *A Guide to Teacher Assessment*, Packs A, B and C, London: SEAC/Heinemann.

SEAC (1990b) *SEAC Recorder*, No. 4, Spring, London: SEAC.

Sedgwick, F. (1989) *Here Comes the Assembly Man*, Lewes: Falmer.

Shayer, M. (1989) 'Can standards in schools be improved?', Paper presented at BERA annual conference, Newcastle, September.

Simon, B. (1988) *Bending the Rules: The Baker 'Reform' of Education*, London: Lawrence and Wishart.

Slee, P.T. (1987) *Child Observation Skills*, London: Croom Helm.

Snowling, M.J. (1985) *Children's Written Language Difficulties*, Windsor: NFER/Nelson.

Solity, J. and Bull, S. (1987) *Special Needs: Bridging the Curriculum Gap*, Milton Keynes: Open University Press.

Stott, D.H. (1978) *Helping Children with Learning Difficulties*, London: Ward Lock Educational.

Sugden, D. (ed.) (1989) *Cognitive Approaches in Special Education*, Lewes: Falmer.

Swann, W. (1988) 'Learning difficulties and curriculum reform: integration or differentiation', pp. 85–107 in G. Thomas and A. Feiler (eds) *Planning for Special Needs: A Whole School Approach*, Oxford: Blackwell.

Swann, W. (1989) *Integration statistics: LEAs reveal local variations*, CSIE (Centre for Studies in Integration Education) Factsheet, London: CSIE.

Sylva, K. and Neill, S. (1990) 'Assessing through direct observation', Unit 2, Warwick University Early Years Team, *Developing your Whole School Approach to Assessment Policy*, Windsor: NFER/Nelson.

Sylva, K., Roy, C. and Painter, M. (1980 *Childwatching at Playgroup and Nursery School*, London: Grant McIntyre.

Tann, S. (1988) 'Grouping and the integrated classroom', pp. 154–70 in G. Thomas and A. Feiler (eds) *Planning for Special Needs: A Whole School Approach*, Oxford: Blackwell.

Tann, S. (1990) 'Assessment-led schooling? Reflections on term 1 of the National Curriculum for five year olds', *Early Years* 10: 2, 9–13.

Thacker, J. (1990) 'Working through groups in the classroom', pp. 68–83 in N. Jones and N. Frederickson, N. (eds) *Refocusing Educational Psychology*, Lewes: Falmer.

Thomas, G. (1988) 'Planning for support in the mainstream', pp.139–53 in G. Thomas and A. Feiler (eds) *Planning for Special Needs: A Whole School Approach*, Oxford: Blackwell.

Thomas, G. and Feiler, A. (eds) (1988) *Planning for Special Needs: A Whole School Approach*, Oxford: Blackwell.

Thomas, N. (1989) Letter, *Child Education*, October 5.

Tilstone, T. and Steel, A. (1989) *The National Curriculum and Severe Learning Difficulties*, West Midlands Monitoring group, Briefing paper 3, Birmingham: Westhill College.

Tizard, B. (1988) 'Test them at five', *Times Educational Supplement*, 20 May.

Tizard, B. and Hughes, M. (1984) *Young Children Learning*, London: Fontana.

Tizard, B., Blatchford, P., Burke, J., Farquar, C. and Plewis, I. (1988) *Young Children at School in the Inner City*, London: Lawrence Erlbaum Associates.

Topping, K. (1988) *The Peer Tutoring Handbook*, London: Croom Helm.

Topping, K. and Wolfendale, S. (1985) *Parental Involvement in Children's Reading*, London: Croom Helm.

Turnbull, J. (1981) *Maths Links*, Stafford: NARE.

Tyler, S. (1990) 'Subtypes of specific learning difficulty: a review', pp. 29–39 in P.D. Pumfrey and C.D. Elliott (eds) *Children's Difficulties in Reading, Spelling and Writing*, Lewes: Falmer.

University of Warwick, Faculty of Educational Studies (1990) Response to draft order: The Education (National Curriculum) (Assessment Arrangements for English, Mathematics and Science) Order 1990.

Ware, J. (1990) 'The National Curriculum for Pupils with Severe Learning Difficulties', pp. 11–18 in H. Daniels and J. Ware (eds) *Special Educational Needs and the National Curriculum*, Bedford Way Series, London: Kogan Page/Institute of Education, University of London.

Warwick University Early Years Team (1990) *Developing your Whole School Approach to Assessment Policy*, Windsor: NFER/Nelson.

Webb, L. (1967) *Children with Special Needs in the Infants' School*, London: Collins.

Wedell, K. (1988) 'The National Curriculum and Special Educational Needs', 102-112 in D. Lawton and C. Chitty (eds) *The National Curriculum*, Bedford Way Paper 33, London: University of London, Institute of Education.

Wedell, K. (1989) 'Children with special educational needs and the National Curriculum', *Education Review* 3: 2, 32–5.

Wedell, K. (1990) 'Overview: The 1988 Act and current principles of special educational needs', pp. 1–10 in H. Daniels and J. Ware (eds) *Special Educational Needs and the National Curriculum*, Bedford Way Series, London: Kogan Page/Institute of Education, University of London.

Wells, G. (1987) *The Meaning Makers*, London: Hodder and Stoughton.

Widlake, P. (1986) *Reducing Educational Disadvantage*, Milton Keynes: Open University Press.

Willes, M. (1983) *Children into Pupils*, London: Routledge and Kegan Paul.

Wilson, D. (1989) 'Integration of a special school: John Watson school', pp. 125–36 in D. Baker and K. Bovair (eds) *Making Special Schools Ordinary* Lewes: Falmer.

WO (Welsh Office) (1988) *Primary School Staffing Survey*, Statistics Bulletin no. 5, Cardiff: Welsh Office.

Wolfendale, S. (1983) *Parental Participation in Children's Education*, London: Gordon and Breach.

Wolfendale, S. (1987 *Primary Schools and Special Needs: Policy, Planning and Provision*, London: Cassell.

Wolfendale, S. (1989) *All About Me*, Polytechnic of North

London/National Children's Bureau.

Wood, D. (1988) *How Children Think and Learn,* Oxford: Blackwell.

Wood, D., McMahon, L. and Cranstoun, Y. (1980) *Working with Under Fives,* London: Grant McIntyre.

Wragg, E.C., Bennett, S.N. and Carre, C.G. (1989) 'Primary teachers and the National Curriculum', *Research Papers in Education* 4: 3, 17–46.

Yapp, N. (1987) *Bluff your Way in Teaching,* Horsham: Ravette.

Name index

ACE (Advisory Centre for Education) 101
AGIT (Advisory Centre for Education/Association for Governor Training) 101
Ainscow, M. 5, 36, 47
Allen, V. L. 88
Alston, J. 44
Archer, M. 48, 91
Arnold, H. 44

Barsby, J. 132–3
Bastinai, J. 107
Bates, S. 83, 153
Beard, R. 40, 41
Beck, K. 95
Bell, G.H. 33
Bennett, N. 40, 88, 91, 153
Berliner, W. 152
Blatchford, P. 15
Blyth, C.A. 123
Boote, R. 47
Bossert, S. 106
Bradley, L. 43
Branwhite, T. 21
Bruce, T. 31, 60
Bryant, P. 43
Bull, S. 21, 47

Calderhead, J. 47
Carpenter, B. 89, 91, 92, 103
Cashdan, A. 40
Cass, A. 91
Cheeseman, R.G. 85

Chrisite, T. 125
Clark, M.M. 84
Cleave, S. 42
Colbeck, B. 33
Conti-Ramsden, G.91
Crocker, A.C. 85
Croft, P. 63
Croll, P. 38, 108
Cronbach, L.J. 3, 49, 82

Daniels, H. 91, 160, 171
Darnbrough, A. 108
David, T. 30. 32
Davies, M. 82
Davies-Jones, G. 48, 113, 135–6
Dawson, R. 36, 108
Dessent, T. 4, 5
Dyson, A. 99

Edwards, A.D. 62, 154
Edwards, D. 155
Elbaz, F. 47
Emblem, B. 91
Evans, L. 52
EYCG (Early years Curriculum Group) 48

Florek, A. 5
Flude, M. 137

Gagné, R.M. 49
Galton, M. 85
Gipps, C. 87, 108
Glynn, T. 89

Subject index